Quick & Easy
Soft Furnishings

Quick & Easy
Soft Furnishings

Janice Bullis

CHANCELLOR
PRESS

A QUANTUM BOOK

This edition published in 2000 by Chancellor Press
An imprint of Bounty Books, a division of
Octopus Publishing Group Ltd
2-4 Heron Quays
London
E14 4JP

ISBN 0-75370-354-8

QUMHEM

This book was produced by
Quantum Publishing
6 Blundell Street
London N7 9BH

Printed in China by Leefung-Asco

CONTENTS

INTRODUCTION

Colour, texture, and pattern are all part of the magic of fabric.

WHETHER YOU WISH to embark on a major redecoration scheme or simply add a few simple soft furnishings to one room, you are sure to find inspiration in this book. The projects are quick and easy to make using a combination of simple sewing and non-sewing techniques, exploiting the newest sewing aids on the market.

Step-by-step instructions are given for all of the projects, which can be completed by those with or without sewing experience. Someone who is already skilled in sewing can learn about and experiment with the latest in sewing techniques, while a person who is just starting to sew can take advantage of the shortcuts without having to worry about the more time-consuming traditional methods.

Choosing fabrics

There are many attractive fabrics available for soft furnishings, and it is often these that inspire people to try their hand at sewing. It is easy to fall in love with a particular fabric – seduced, perhaps, by its luscious colour, interesting pattern or cool, crisp texture. But before you select it for a project, you should first consider some practical matters.

The two most important considerations in choosing the right fabric are fibre content and the way the fabric is constructed. The fibre is spun into yarn, and the yarn is made into fabric; how this yarn is woven (or sometimes knitted) will determine how durable the fabric is.

The fibre can be natural – that is, derived from plants or animals; cotton, linen, silk and wool are natural fibres. Or it can be synthetic – that is, produced from chemicals; polyester, nylon and acetate are synthetic fibres. Each fibre has distinctive qualities, which determine its suitability for different uses. Some of these qualities are negative: cotton, for example, has a reputation for shrinking, acetate for losing its colour and linen for creasing easily. However, it is possible to blend two or more fibres in a fabric, thus counterbalancing their good and bad properties. Alternatively, the manufacturer can apply a finish to the fabric to add body, prevent fading or discourage creasing.

The type of weave will determine the durability of the fabric.

Match the density of the fabric you choose to its intended use. For example, fabric for chair covers will need to be very hard-wearing, whereas bed covers can be made of less durable materials.

Furnishing fabrics Most furnishing fabrics are woven, as this method of construction is more stable than knitting. The type and density of the weave determine the durability of the fabric. For instance, a lightweight fabric made from fine yarns woven densely may well prove to be more durable than a heavy fabric made from loosely woven yarns.

Other fabrics Fabric designed for clothing can be used for some soft furnishing projects. These fabrics are usually lighter in weight and narrower than furnishing fabrics but can be suitable for some informal curtains and accessories.

Sheets and readymade duvet covers can often substitute effectively for furnishing fabric, and their use is suggested in several projects. They are now available in an amazing variety of pretty designs and are economical and easy to care for. In addition, the extra-wide width and readymade hems can cut sewing time in half.

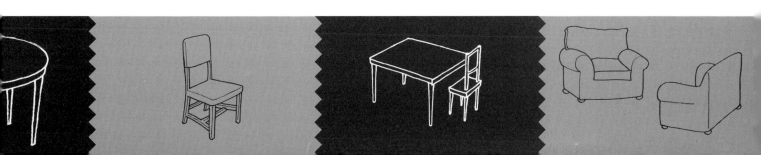

Variations on a theme: experiment with different styles and materials before making your final choice.

Instructions for caring for the fabric can often be found on the label (if not, ask the sales assistant). The amount of wear or dirt to which the finished project will be subjected should be taken into account. For instance, kitchen curtains will need frequent cleaning and should be made of a washable fabric, whereas sitting-room curtains will need only the occasional dry cleaning. The bed covering in a child's bedroom will probably need a crease-resistant and stain-repellent finish, whereas that on a seldom-used guest bed may not.

How much fabric In some of the projects in this book the required fabric amount has been specified. In others, the amount will depend on your own requirements – for example, on the size of bed or window for which the project is intended. Read through the project instructions first, and draw a plan including the relevant measurements. Take this to the shop and use it as a basis for calculating the amount of fabric to buy. Make sure to allow for pattern repeats and possible shrinkage. A calculator is also useful, although the sales assistant can usually be called on for help in calculating the required amount.

There is a wealth of fabric designs to choose from; colour and texture can be similar or complementary.

Draped, swagged or stretched over screens, fabric creates atmosphere. Choose accessories to match or to contrast.

'Sewing' without thread The latest inventions in sewing technology include products that have little to do with needle and thread. It is now possible to join two pieces of fabric by gluing or fusing them together. Such materials as interfacing and some curtain tapes can also often be applied with adhesives rather than by sewing.

Once you have learned the techniques and become familiar with the use of these products through the projects in this book, you can go on to experiment with using them for ideas of your own. By all means, make use of the basic sewing techniques where appropriate, but don't be afraid to break with tradition.

Whatever the project, try to approach it in a pragmatic, innovative spirit. If it makes sense to fuse, rather than stitch, the hems of your curtains – why not? If a sheet has the perfect colour and pattern for your kitchen, make it into some quilted placemats and matching napkins. Turn an exquisite lace runner into a pillow cover. You may be surprised at how much fun sewing (and non-sewing!) can be.

Contrasting patterns can produce luxurious effects.

Curtain rings come in various styles and materials. Choose to suit the effect you want.

BEFORE YOU BEGIN

Each project includes a list of basic techniques required to complete it. All of these techniques are described here. You should first read through this section to familiarise yourself with the equipment and techniques; then, when making a specific project, you can refer to a certain technique if necessary. In every case we have chosen the techniques that are most suited to making the project quick, easy and fun to execute.

MEASURING UP

It is important that your measurements are full and accurate. All the measurements you need for the projects in this book are included here.

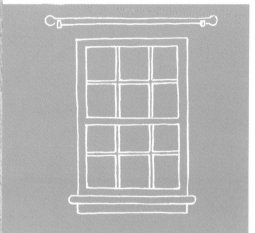

WINDOWS

For the best results when making curtains or other window treatments, you should fix the pole, rod or mounting board first, before calculating fabric amounts. This will enable you to cut and hem the panels accurately.

Measuring the width To purchase the appropriate length of pole or mounting board, you must first decide whether the curtains or blind should be fixed inside or outside the window frame. For an inside mount, measure between the inside edges of the window frame. An inside mount may not be possible for windows positioned more or less flush with the wall.

For an outside mount, attach the brackets to the wall, rather than to the window frame. It may be desirable to use a pole long enough so that the curtains, when open, will stack back on the wall to expose all of the glass. Measure the desired distance to each side from the outside of the window frame – anywhere from 5cm to 45cm (2in to 18in) may be required.

Measure the length of the mounted pole, then determine the required fullness of the fabric. Depending upon the project, the finished fabric width can be equal to the pole length (as in the case of a roller blind, for example) or up to three times the length (for full net curtains, for example). The fullness is often expressed as a ratio; for example, a ratio of 2:1 means that the curtain is twice the width of the pole.

Measuring the length Mount the pole or board 2.5cm–10cm (1in–4in) above the top edge of the window frame. Measure the distance from the top of the pole or mounting board to the required position of the lower edge of the window treatment: at the sill, below the apron (lower part of sill), or to the floor. The calculations for each project take into consideration casings (which fit over the rod), headings, and hems. All floor-length draperies finish 1.2cm (½in) above the floor.

Installing window treatments The construction of the wall or window frame will determine the type of hardware needed to mount a curtain pole or mounting board brackets. Be sure to anchor the rod or board securely for heavy curtains or a treatment to which extra strain will be applied when raising and lowering.

After the pole or board is mounted, measure its length between the brackets. Also, using a tape measure, measure the circumference of a curtain pole for a casing. You should normally allow a little extra to this measurement when calculating the size of the casing, so that the fabric will glide smoothly over the pole. To test the effect, cut a strip of fabric to the estimated size of the casing and slip it over the pole. Additional fabric should be allowed for the heading above the casing.

A mounting board can be used either inside or outside the window frame. To camouflage the board, you can paint it a colour similar to the fabric or wrap the entire board in fabric, depending upon how much of the board will be visible. Mount it with L brackets to the moulding for an inside mount or to the wall for an outside mount.

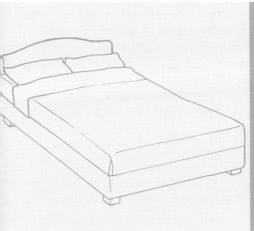
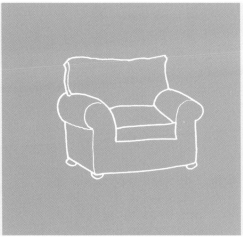
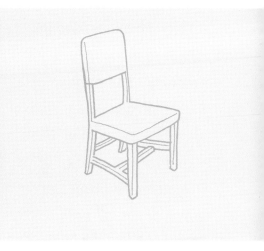

BEDS

Although most beds are manufactured in standard sizes, it is best to measure the bed itself to be sure of accuracy. Measure the width and length of the bed across the mattress.

Measure the thickness of the mattress. Measure the height of the box spring from the floor and the height of the mattress from the floor. The finished size of the project can be determined from these measurements.

Standard British mattress sizes

Single	90cm × 190cm (3ft × 6ft 3in)
Double	135cm × 190cm (4ft 6in × 6ft 3in)
Queen	150cm × 200cm (5ft × 6ft 6in)
King	180cm × 200cm (6ft × 6ft 6in)

British pillow sizes

Standard	48cm × 74cm (19in × 29in)
King	48cm × 92cm (19in × 36in)
Square	65cm × 65cm (26in × 26in)

PILLOWS

Bed pillows are also available in standard sizes, but because of the wide variety in the methods of construction, it is best to measure the pillow from seam to seam. Measure scatter cushions in the same way.

CHAIRS

When measuring an armchair or sofa, it is important to remember to be generous with the measurements. A little bit of fabric is used up every time it dips around a seat or cushion or rolls over an arm. Pinning or tacking the seams before they are sewn will help to customise the fit.

Dining chairs For square or rectangular seats, measure the length and width of the seat. For those chair seats that narrow towards the back or are a unique shape, place paper over the seat and trace the shape. Measure the depth and perimeter of the seat cushion. Add seam and hem allowances where necessary.

Sofas and armchairs Measure the width of the sofa from the floor in front, up to the seat, across the seat to the back, up the back and down again to the floor in back of the sofa. Measure the length of the sofa from the floor at one side, up over the shoulder, across the back, over the other shoulder and down to the floor again. Be generous, not conservative, with these measurements, as any excess fabric can be tucked into the gap of the chair between the seat cushion and inside arm. For the armchair, take these same width and length measurements with the cushion removed; measure the width, length and depth of the cushion separately. Piece together panels of fabric and add seam and hem allowances where necessary.

TABLES

Measure the width and length or the diameter of the table top. Measure the height of the table from the edge to the floor or to the seat of the chair.

JOINING FABRIC WIDTHS

A single fabric width is often narrower than the width of the item you are making. The number of widths needed, the method of cutting and joining them and the importance of matching a printed or woven design all need to be considered at the outset.

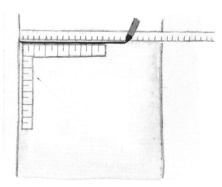

Grain This is the direction of the threads in a woven fabric. The lengthwise grain of the fabric runs parallel to the selvedge, or finished edge. The crosswise grain runs at a right angle to it. If the fabric needs to be cut along the lengthwise grain, measure the required distance from the selvedge at two or more points, mark these points and join them to make a line parallel to the selvedge. If the fabric is to be cut along the crosswise grain, line up one leg of a carpenter's square along the selvedge; the adjacent leg will follow the crosswise grain.

Before buying fabric, make sure that the two grains run correctly at right angles to each other. Most

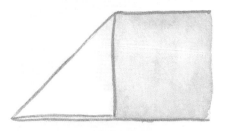

good-quality furnishing fabrics do, but if the cut edge shows the crosswise threads running diagonally to the selvedge, it is probably unwise to buy it.

Bias This refers to the 45-degree angle that runs between the lengthwise and crosswise grains. To find the bias, fold the fabric so that the two grains are aligned.

Woven fabric is stable along both grain lines, without much give; but when it is pulled along the bias, it stretches. Cut fabric along the bias when extra stretch is needed – for example, to make bias tape or strips to cover cord. Also see ***Making and applying trimmings.***

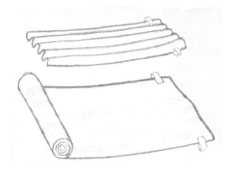

Directional fabrics If the fabric has a one-way design (one that looks different when viewed from the two ends) or a nap (a raised surface), pieces should be cut and joined so that the design or nap runs in the same direction, where appropriate. When making curtains, for example, mark the top of each fabric width before joining the widths. It is easy enough to determine the direction on some fabrics – e.g. one printed with standing birds; a piece with the birds upside down would be readily apparent. Less obvious are busy florals, geometrics, asymmetrical stripes, some checks and fabrics with a nap. To avoid confusion, mark lengths of directional fabric with tape or a safety pin at the top as they are cut.

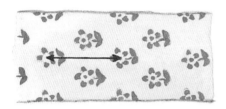

Repeats The design of a printed, striped or checked fabric repeats at regular intervals. The length of this repeat should be taken into consideration before purchasing and cutting, as described below. In most cases the repeat distance is given on the label. If it is not, measure from the centre of a prominent motif, along the lengthwise grain to the centre of the next identical motif. Make a note of the measurement.

Matching the pattern When joining pieces of patterned fabric, you will need to match the pattern repeat at the seams. Regardless of the fabric width, a quality furnishing fabric is designed so that the pattern can be matched at the seams with no unsightly break in the print, even when several widths

are sewn together.

You will probably have enough fabric to be able not only to match the design but also to take full seam allowances and trim away and discard the selvedges. Some fabric at the top or bottom of each piece must often be wasted in order to match the design. In order to be sure you are purchasing enough fabric, add the repeat measurement to every length you need. For a large design repeat you may need to add as much as 70cm (¾yd) for every length needed. At first, the extra expenditure may seem unnecessary and wasteful, but the importance of cutting the pieces in this way will soon become evident.

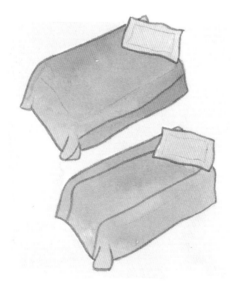

Balancing The finished width of the project will determine how many fabric lengths will be needed. Their positioning should be planned carefully. As a general rule, whole fabric widths should be placed at the

centre of a project and partial widths at the sides, to avoid centre seams. Any partial widths must be equal to ensure symmetry. This balancing is equally important for solid-coloured fabric with no design repeat.

For a one-piece project, such as a duvet cover, allow a whole width at the centre and split one or trim from two whole widths at the sides.

For a two-piece project, such as a pair of curtains, place a whole width at the inner edge of each panel and a partial width (if necessary) at the outer edges.

For some projects, a whole width at the centre may be too wide. This often happens with bed covers when only a narrow strip is necessary on each side to make up the full width, resulting in seams very near the edges – a clear indication of their piecing function. To make the seams appear part of the project's design, trim some fabric from the sides of the centre piece and cut the side pieces correspondingly wider.

If the fabric has a printed or woven pattern, you will need to experiment – before cutting the project to size – to match the pattern at the seams. Allow a whole extra repeat when cutting the centre piece and do not trim it at the sides. Then move the side pieces along it at the chosen positions for the seams until the pattern matches. Seam the sections together and trim the centre piece as required.

MAKING PATTERNS AND CUTTING SHAPES

Home furnishing projects seldom require a paper pattern. They normally consist of simple shapes, such as rectangles or circles, which can be marked directly on the fabric. However, sometimes you may find it convenient to make a paper pattern first – if, for example, a shape is relatively complex or if several identical fabric pieces must be cut, in which case marking them individually would entail extra work. Simply mark the shapes on the paper as specified in the project instructions. Add seam allowances where necessary. Pin the pattern to the fabric and cut around it.

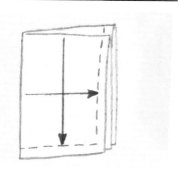

Rectangles and squares It is important that squares and rectangles have all adjacent sides at right angles to each other. To achieve a right angle, place a carpenter's square or set square along the lengthwise grain of the fabric and then measure the desired width and length from each of the legs of the square.

Due to the size of some projects, it is sometimes difficult to measure and cut accurately – even the floor may not be big enough. In such a case, the solution is to cut pieces slightly longer and wider than required, join the seams, then trim the edges as follows. Fold the seamed fabric in half widthwise and then in half again lengthwise, keeping all the cut edges even. Measuring from the two adjacent folded edges, determine the cutting size by dividing each dimension – length and width – in half. (Remember to add outer seam/hem allowance). This method requires less space and with careful measurement can be just as accurate.

Circles For circular patterns, begin with a square cut to the diameter of the circle, including seam/hem allowance. Fold the fabric in half twice, matching all cut edges. Pin the layers together at the edges. Divide the diameter by 2 to get the radius. Using a tape measure as a compass, measure and mark the radius from the folded corner at frequent intervals. (Place a heavy object at the corner to hold the tape in place for each mark). Join the marks in a curved line, then cut through all the layers along this line. Unfold the fabric for a perfect circle.

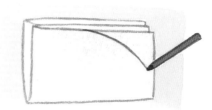

Ovals For oval patterns, begin with a rectangle cut to the desired outer dimensions. Fold the fabric in half lengthwise and in half again crosswise, matching all cut edges. Locate the open corner (without folds) and, measuring the two adjacent sides, mark a curved line along it. (It can be a good idea to make a paper pattern to ensure a smooth, well-proportioned curve.) Cut through all the layers along the marked line.

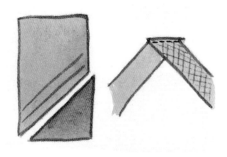

MAKING AND APPLYING TRIMMINGS

Braid, cord, bias tape, lace and ribbon are all readily available in hundreds of styles and colours to give a finishing touch to your decorating project. With a little more investment in time, you can make your own trimmings from fabric. Bias tape is made from narrow strips of fabric cut on the bias; these can also be used to cover a piping cord to make piping. Stitch the strips together following the fabric grain to achieve the length needed.

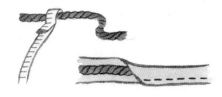

Piping To make piping, first measure the circumference of the piping cord and add seam allowances. The total is the cutting width of the strips. Fold the strips

around the cord and stitch close to the cord, using the zipper foot on the machine.

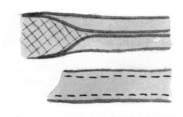

Single-fold bias tape To make a single-fold bias tape, allow twice the finished width when cutting. Place the strip wrong side up on the ironing board, and turn in the edges so that they meet in the centre; press. Stitch the tape flat to the project along each fold.

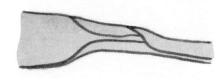

Double-fold bias tape To make double-fold bias tape, allow four times the finished width. Press the strip lengthwise, as for single-fold tape, with the cut edges meeting in the centre. Then fold the strip in half down the centre, enclosing the cut edges. The tape is applied to the edge of the fabric as a practical seam finish or decorative trimming.

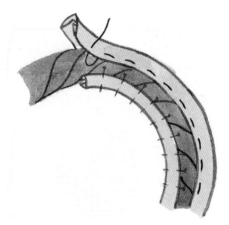

Applying tape To apply the tape to curves, stretch the outer edges slightly and shrink the inner edge with steam from an iron, easing it around the curve. Hold the tape in place with plenty of pins, or tacking, then stitch flat.

To mitre a corner, when applying a single-fold tape, first stitch the tape to the position of the corner along both edges; then break the stitching and fold the tape diagonally to form a right angle. Resume stitching along the adjacent edges.

To mitre double-fold tape when binding an edge, stitch through all layers up to the corner, and break off the stitching. Fold the tape back on itself on the front and the back. Pin the folds in place securely, then resume stitching.

GENERAL SEWING EQUIPMENT

All the equipment necessary to complete the projects is listed here. You should be able to buy any of the items in your local needlecraft shop or department store.

MEASURING EQUIPMENT

Tape measure A flexible tape measure that will not stretch is an essential tool.

Spring-return metal tape This extra-long tape measure is helpful for large projects.

Metre rule or yardstick A good non-flexible measuring tool which is also useful for marking straight edges.

Carpenter's square or **set square** Either of these can be used to measure right angles; some set squares will also measure 45-degree angles.

Seam gauge A small ruler with a sliding marker is helpful when marking small distances, as for seams and hems.

Magnetic seam guide A sewing machine attachment to ensure a uniform and accurate seam width. It is easily adjusted for sewing wider headings and hems.

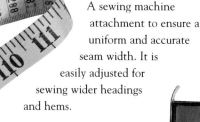

MARKING EQUIPMENT

Fabric-marking pencil Also known as a quilter's pencil, this is a readily visible and easy-to-remove method of marking fabric. A few colours will suffice for all fabrics.

Tailor's chalk A temporary marking method suitable for some fabrics. Chalk is available in pencil form, by the piece, or as loose powder in a plastic holder.

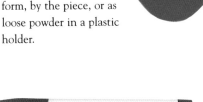

Air-soluble pen A pen filled with ink that evaporates after a period of time. It is ideal for temporary markings.

Water-soluble pen A pen filled with ink that can be removed with a damp cloth. It is good to use on washable fabrics and for markings that need to remain over the course of a few days or weeks.

Tracing wheel and paper Useful for transferring pattern markings to fabric. The marks may be permanent or temporary, depending on the brand.

Note Before using any marking material, test it on a scrap of the fabric.

CUTTING EQUIPMENT

Dressmakers' shears These long-bladed scissors have handles shaped to fit the hand, with openings for a thumb on one side and for several fingers on the other. The angle between blades and handles makes them ideal for cutting fabric placed flat on a table.

Sewing scissors These are useful for trimming seam allowances, clipping curves and many other jobs.

Pinking shears One of the fastest methods of neatening a seam to prevent fraying. Because of the variation in width that they produce, they are not intended for cutting out the fabric.

Stitch unpicker Used for safely removing stitching mistakes and machine tacking stitches. Available in large and small sizes.

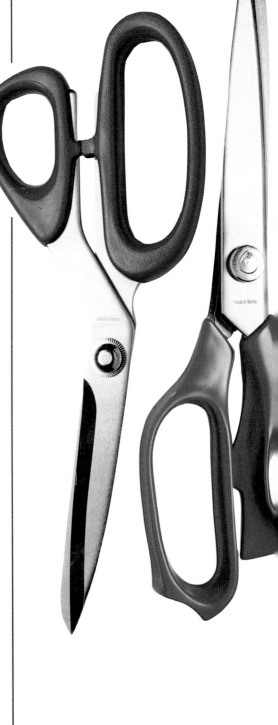

Hand and machine needles Choose the size and type according to the fibre content and number of layers of fabric. Choose sewing thread following the same guidelines.

Pins Extra-long pins, especially those with large ball or T-shaped heads, are the best choice for heavier furnishing fabrics.

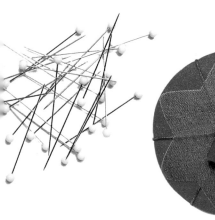

Pincushion A useful container for holding pins. Some fit on the wrist for convenience.

Thimble Protects the middle fingertip when hand sewing; especially useful when sewing thick fabrics.

Bodkins These come in different styles, including one resembling tweezers with locking teeth. It grabs the end of a length of elastic or ribbon and is then used to pull it through a stitched casing. A large safety pin can serve the same purpose.

Quilter's bicycle clips These large spring-form rings hold a rolled-up section of a quilt, making the opposite end easier to work on and the size of the project more manageable.

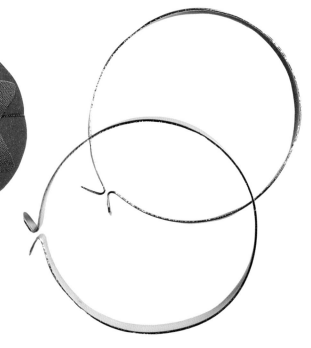

Iron For pressing creases from fabric, pressing seams, creasing folds and hems, and applying most fusing webs and interfacing.

Seam roll Originally designed for tailoring, this tool is helpful in home furnishing projects for pressing seams. It is inserted in tubular shapes and placed on the ironing board; the seam can then be pressed without creasing the fabric.

FUSING MATERIALS

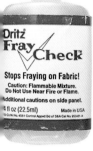

Seam sealant A liquid applied to the cut edge of woven fabric to prevent raveling.

Permanent adhesive A liquid white glue designed specifically for fabric.

Fusing web strips
Fabric adhesive that resembles a strip of netting. It is used to bond two layers of fabric together, or fabric to a porous surface such as cardboard. The adhesive melts when heat from an iron is applied to the fabric. It is available in several widths, as a permanent or temporary adhesive, and with or without a paper backing.

Glue stick This adhesive is useful for holding edges together before they are stitched, and so serves the same purpose as tacking. It will wash out.

Fusing web sheets Similar to fusing web strips but much wider.

FILLERS

Wadding The filler between two layers of fabric in a quilt or comforter. It is available in many thicknesses and sizes.

Cushion pads Preformed shapes of feather-filled fabric are available in a wide range of sizes and several shapes. Pads made of foam are also available from some suppliers, often by special order.

BASIC STITCHING TECHNIQUES

The various stitches used in the projects are very simple, but it is important to use the right stitch for the right task. All the stitches and their uses are described here.

The large size and the long straight lines of most home furnishing projects dictate that almost all of the seaming, hemming and finishing is machine-sewn rather than hand-sewn. It is also this simplicity of design that makes these projects ideal for fusing and gluing materials. Before you decide whether to stitch or fuse a project, or part of a project, together, see **When to sew and when to fuse (pp. 24–25).**

Straight stitching This stitch, which forms a thin, solid line, is the one you will normally use, especially for seams. Unless otherwise instructed, you should allow 1.2cm (½in) seam allowance throughout. Once stitched, the seam should be pressed open, even if it will later be pressed to one side. This initial pressing helps to embed the stitches in the fabric and give a crisp finish. In some cases you will need to trim the seam allowance to reduce bulk. Also clip the excess from corners and curved seams.

Zigzag stitching A line of zigzag stitch is an ideal way to neaten seam allowances. Worked close to the raw edge, the stitches will prevent the fabric from continuing to fray. (Some fabrics do not require neatening, and it is not necessary for items that are fully lined). A zigzag stitch is also used to stitch appliqués by machine. For a dense stitch that covers the edges of the motif completely – called satin stitch – set the stitch as short and as wide as possible.

Buttons, traditionally sewn on by hand, are easily sewn by machine on a zigzag setting with the feed dog (teeth) of the machine disengaged. See your machine instruction manual for details.

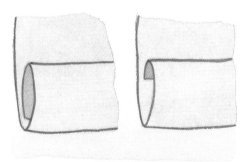

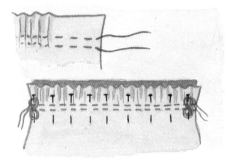

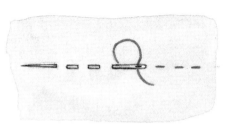

Hemming Unless otherwise instructed, always plan for a double hem in soft furnishing projects. Besides giving the project a professional-looking finish, this helps to give the fabric weight and makes it more drapable – especially desirable in curtains.

It also makes the hem appear uniform. Choose a single hem when you need to minimise bulk or when an applied trimming will provide the necessary weight.

Gathering with machine tacking
A long straight machine stitch is one way of gathering fabric for frills. You can either work one row within the seam allowance, or two rows straddling the seamline. When the stitching is complete, pull up the bobbin thread to form the gathering. Secure the thread ends around pins, then adjust the gathers evenly and pin the frill in place.

Because most furnishing fabrics are relatively heavy, and gathering may need to be worked over long distances, placing a strain on the stitching, it is a good idea to use a heavy-duty thread for this purpose. Wind the heavy thread on the bobbin and use ordinary thread on the needle. When you come to pull the bobbin thread to gather the fabric, it is less likely to break.

Machine tacking A long straight stitch, this helps to hold fabrics, interfacings or trimmings in place until the permanent stitching can be done. Some machines will do an extra-long stitch, 1.2cm (½in) long, for this purpose.

Tacking by hand When joining fabric layers temporarily, it is sometimes easiest to use a long running stitch instead of pins, which can slip out, or machine tacking, which is impractical if the item is very unwieldy.

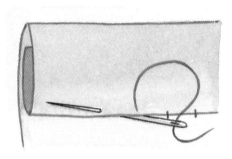

Slipstitch This stitch is used where it is not possible to use the machine and where fabrics and/or trimmings need to be joined invisibly. The needle catches a few fabric threads of one layer, then goes through the adjacent folded edge (or simply under a finished edge, as in braid, for example) and up, then back into the other fabric layer.

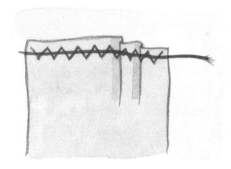

Gathering over cord For a slightly stronger gathering method, zigzag over a lightweight cord placed within the seam allowance. Pull the cord to gather the fabric.

WHEN TO SEW AND WHEN TO FUSE

The fusible materials and fabric glues now readily available are ideal for many home-furnishing projects, so that even those with little sewing experience can complete them successfully.

Fusing web

The best choice for turning up hems is narrow strips of fusing web, usually sold on rolls. Some of these strips have a paper backing, which makes application a two-step process; this allows for greater accuracy.

The great advantage of hemming with fusing web is that no stitches show on the right side. Using web strips to apply ribbon helps to keep it flat. The strips can even be used for seaming, provided that no stress will be applied to the seam.

Fusing web is also available in wide sheets. Web with temporary adhesive is excellent for holding the edges of an intricate appliqué motif in place until it is sewn. Web with permanent adhesive can be used to bond layers without the need for sewing, even if the item is to be laundered many times.

Fusing fabrics

All manufacturers of fusing web provide specific instructions for applying its products, though these can differ greatly from one manufacturer to the next, even for the same type of web. All webs are applied with an ordinary household iron; the major difference lies in whether or not the manufacturer recommends the use of steam. Webs with a removable paper backing may require a dry iron for the first stage and a steam iron after the paper is removed. Other differences include the temperature setting and the amount of time and pressure needed. For the best results, always follow the manufacturer's instructions carefully, and test the web on a scrap of fabric to see how the two react.

Fabric glue

Fabric glue, also known as PVA glue, is permanent and strong and best used in small areas, especially those that will be subject to added stress. Use it, for example, to hold the corner of a seam that may come under strain. It is also useful for applying bulky trimming that may be difficult to

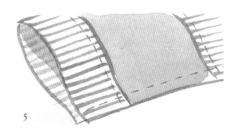

sew. Look for glue that remains soft and pliable while you are working with it. The glue also should not bleed through or discolour the fabric.

A liquid seam sealant is the chemical way to neaten cut edges. It bonds the fibres together to prevent the cut edge of the fabric from fraying, yet without impairing the fabric's soft texture.

Interfacing

The purpose of interfacing is to add body to a fabric – a job that fusible, or iron-on, interfacing does very well, provided the area is not too large, in which case the interfacing may be difficult to apply smoothly. It is ideal along the heading or hem of a curtain panel and on accessories. Fusible interfacing comes in several weights, which produce noticeably different effects. Always test the interfacing with a large scrap of your fabric before using it in the project.

Curtain heading tape

The newest product to be offered in fusing form is curtain heading tape. This has pre-measured folds and stitched-in cords and pockets, which allow the tape to be stitched or fused in place while flat. The fabric can then be pleated by drawing the cords. The tape is applied with an iron and then allowed to cool; it is then reheated to make the cords easier to draw or to ease the insertion of the curtain hooks.

When to sew

The fusible products described above are generally marketed as convenient, time-saving alternatives to sewing. Although this is true in many cases, in others it is quicker and easier to sew than to fuse. For instance, if a seam does not lie flat on the ironing board, attempting to fuse it can be a tricky operation. Also, if a seam or hem is very long, you may find that continually positioning the web and fusing it in place over short stretches can become very tedious and time consuming. With experience you will learn when it makes sense to use a machine instead.

1 Fusible web: for hems and appliqué.
2 Fabric glue: for small areas, or areas of added strain.
3 Quilt interfacing: adds body to the fabric.
4 Drapery construction tape: can be stitched or fused in place while flat.
5 Sewing: sometimes it is quicker and easier to sew than to fuse.

EASY LIVING

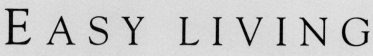

Table top accessories are the perfect choice for quick and easy decorating and in many cases require only a small amount of fabric. Choose them for a special occasion or when you want to make an ordinary day seem special. Pelmets, whether frilled or flat, require only a small amount of fabric to soften and add colour to an angular frame. Also in this chapter you will find an alternative to time-consuming tailored loose covers – wrap-and-tie casual loose covers – that are appealing and easy to make.

TABLE ACCESSORIES

Combine the simplicity of linen with the delicacy of lace to create an elegant table setting.

C H E C K L I S T

Materials

(for one runner, one placemat, one napkin)
1.4m (4½ft) of 115cm (45in) wide linen fabric
70cm (28in) of 115cm (45in) wide iron-on interfacing
6.4m (21ft) of 3.5cm (1¼in) wide flat lace trim
3 heart-shaped lace doilies, 25cm (10in) in diameter
General sewing equipment
Liquid seam sealant
Paper for pattern

Techniques

Making patterns	pp. 16–17
Applying trimmings	pp. 16–17
Machine stitching	pp. 22–23
Hand stitching	pp. 22–23

Cutting the patterns

Placemat From the pattern paper, measure and cut a rectangle 33cm x 48cm (13in x 19in).
Napkin Measure and cut a square 46cm x 46cm (18in x 18in).
Runner Measure and cut a rectangle 33cm x 112cm (13in x 44in). Measure and mark the centre point on each short edge, then mark 18cm (7in) from the end of each long side. Cut along these lines to form two points. Sizes include 1.2cm (½in) seam allowances.

1 Using the pattern pieces, cut two placemats, two runners and one napkin from the fabric. Cut one placemat and one runner from the interfacing. Trim 1.2cm (½in) from the edges of the interfacing pieces.

2 Following the manufacturer's instructions, carefully fuse each piece of interfacing to the wrong side of one corresponding fabric piece.

3 Place the two placemat pieces together with right sides facing and edges even. Pin and then stitch them together, leaving a 15cm (6in) opening along one long edge.

5 Pin the heart doily to the centre of the placemat. Topstitch the doily in place around the edge. If the edge is intricate, secure the points with fabric glue.

4 Trim the seams and cut across the corners. Press and turn right side out. Slipstitch the opening edges together and press the placemat flat.

6 Starting in the centre of the lower edge, pin the lace trim around the edge of the placemat on the right side. Lap the straight edge of the lace over the fabric edge. Stitch it in place with two lines of topstitching, turning under the finishing end to conceal the starting end. Topstitch the corners along the fold.

To complete the table runner

7 Follow the placemat steps 2–5, substituting two heart doilies at each end for the one in the centre.

To complete the napkin

8 Turn under and press 1.2cm (½in) on all four edges. Tuck the cut edge in to meet the fold and press again. Topstitch the double hem along the inside fold.

9 Pin the doily to one corner of the napkin so that it overlaps the edges attractively. Topstitch the doily edges in place, using either zigzag stitch or two rows of straight stitching; take the threads to the wrong side and knot them together securely. Trim away the fabric from under the doily along the stitching line. For added security, apply a liquid seam sealant to prevent fraying of the cut edge.

To make this project simpler, apply the heart-shaped doilies with fabric glue, and use pinking shears to give an attractive zigzag edge which needs no hemming.

BORDERED CLOTH

Brighten up your next buffet supper with a bordered tablecloth and matching napkins.

C H E C K L I S T

Materials

2 coordinating furnishing fabrics, one with stripes
General sewing equipment
Paper-backed 1cm (⅜in)-wide fusing web strip

Techniques

Measuring up: tables	pp. 12–13
Joining fabric widths	pp. 14–15
Machine stitching	pp. 12–13
Fusing fabric	pp. 24–25

Measuring up

Measure the width and length of the table. Measure the drop from the edge of the table to the top of the chair seat.

Cutting sizes

Cloth For the cutting width, multiply the drop by 2, then add the table width plus 2.5cm (1in). For the cutting length, multiply the drop by 2, then add the table length plus 2.5cm (1in). Piece widths of fabric together if necessary to achieve the dimensions of the tablecloth.
Borders For the cutting width, select a section of the striped fabric measuring approximately 8cm–10cm (3in–4in) in width; measure it and add 2.5cm (1in). The cutting length of each border is equal to the cutting width or length of the cloth.
Napkin Cut these 41cm (16in) square.
Cutting sizes include 1.2cm (½in) hem allowance.

1 Following the cutting dimensions, cut one cloth from the main furnishing fabric and two short borders and two long borders from the striped fabric. Cut one square from the striped fabric for each napkin.

2 On one long edge of each border piece, turn the fabric under and press 1.2cm (½in).

3 Pin a short border to a long border, placing the right sides together and matching the cut ends and the folded edges.

4 Keeping the pinned ends even, lift the top border and position it at right angles to the bottom border. Press the diagonal fold.

5 Pin and stitch the borders together along the crease of the diagonal fold, backstitching at the ends to secure. Trim the seam 5mm (¼in) from the stitching line and press it open.

6 Repeat steps 3–5 to join the other two borders, taking care to join them in the correct order.

7 Following the manufacturer's instructions, apply fusing web to the folded hem allowance on the inner edge of the border. Do not remove the paper backing.

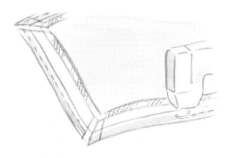

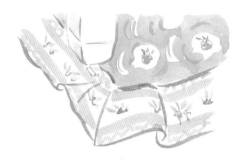

11► Turn under and press 1.2cm (½in) on all edges of the napkin. Tuck the cut edge in to meet the fold, and press again. Topstitch the double hem along the inside fold, or secure it with fusing web.

8► Place the border, right side down, on the wrong side of the cloth with cut edges even. Pin the border to the cloth along the outer edges. Stitch together, taking 1.2cm (½in) seam allowance. Trim the seam and clip diagonally across the corners.

10► Remove the paper backing and fuse the border to the cloth. Topstitch through all the layers close to the inner edge of the border.

The cloth is hemmed and the border applied in the same step. Perfectly mitred corners are easy to achieve with a simple fold, press and stitch method, which eliminates calculations and guesswork. This design is for a rectangular or square table.

9► Press the seam open, reaching as far into the corners as possible, then turn the border to the right side of the cloth. Push out the corners to make them sharp, and along the outer edge.

TABLECLOTH SET

Perfect for the kitchen or patio, this geranium-print tablecloth and coordinating skirt add colour to a room.

C H E C K L I S T

Materials

2 coordinating furnishing fabrics
General sewing equipment
Fusing web strip, 1.2cm (½in) wide
Adhesive 2-cord shirring tape

Techniques

Measuring up: tables	pp. 12–13
Joining fabric widths	pp. 14–15
Cutting the shapes: circles	pp. 16–17
Machine stitching	pp. 22–23

Measuring up

Measure the height of the table and the diameter of the table top.

Cutting sizes

Table skirt For the cutting width, add twice the table height to the table diameter; add 5cm (2in). Piece several widths of fabric together if necessary to achieve the correct width. The cutting length is identical to the width.

Tablecloth For the cutting width, divide the height by 1.5; add the diameter plus 5cm (2in). The cutting length is identical to the width. The cutting dimensions allow the finished table skirt to clear the floor by 1.2cm (½in). The tablecloth will overhang the table by one-third the height.

1 Using the measurements you have made, cut the larger square from the table skirt fabric and the smaller one from the tablecloth fabric.

To complete the table skirt

2 Fold the cloth in half crosswise and in half again lengthwise. Measure off half the cutting width; this is the radius of the circle. Place the end of the tape measure at the folded corner. Using the tape as a compass, mark a quarter circle on the cloth. Cut along this line through all layers.

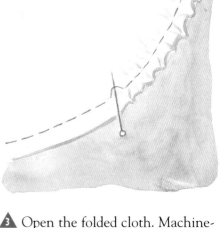

3 Open the folded cloth. Machine-tack 5mm (¼in) from the edge. Approximately every 15cm (6in) insert a pin under a tacking stitch and gently lift until the fabric gathers slightly.

4 Turn under and press 2.5cm (1in) around the edge. Relax or tighten the tacking stitches as required for evenly distributed fullness. Tuck the cut edge in to meet the fold, and press again, hiding the tacking stitches. Following the manufacturer's instructions, use the fusing web strip to fuse the double hem in place.

To complete the tablecloth

5 Repeat steps 2–4 to cut and hem the tablecloth circle.

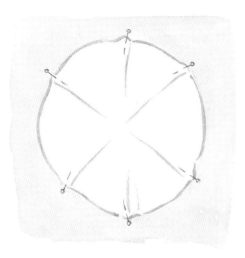

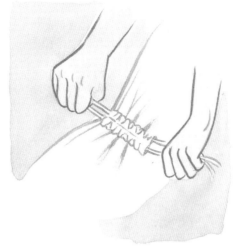

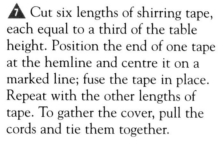

Fusing web and an iron are all you need for quick and easy hems if the material you are using has not been finished on the edges.

6 Fold the cloth in half, then fold it again into thirds. Mark the edges with pins at the folds. On the wrong side of the fabric, use a metre rule and marking pen to draw three lines between opposite points, dividing the circle into six equal segments.

7 Cut six lengths of shirring tape, each equal to a third of the table height. Position the end of one tape at the hemline and centre it on a marked line; fuse the tape in place. Repeat with the other lengths of tape. To gather the cover, pull the cords and tie them together.

APPLIQUED PICNIC BASKET

When fusing web is used, appliqués of any shape are quick and easy.

CHECKLIST

Materials

Coordinating furnishing fabrics
1cm (⅜in)-wide piping cord
Picnic basket
Thick card
Lightweight wadding
Paper-backed fusing web
Fabric glue
General sewing equipment

Techniques

Making patterns and cutting shapes pp. 16–17
Machine stitching   pp. 22–23
Applying trimmings   pp. 16–17
Fusing fabric   pp. 24–25

Measuring up

Measure the width, length and perimeter of the picnic basket lid.

Cutting sizes

Fabric Cover For the cutting dimensions, add 7.5cm (3in) to the measured length and width.
Piping Strip The cutting width is 5cm (2in). The length is the same as the perimeter of the lid plus about 5cm (2in). Piece several fabric widths together, if necessary.
Wadding and Card For the cutting dimensions, trace the lid of the basket.
Fruit and Fusing Web For the cutting dimensions, cut a rectangle approximately 1.2cm (½in) greater on all edges than each appliqué motif.

1▶ Following the cutting dimensions, cut one fabric cover, one piping strip, one wadding piece and one card piece.

2▶ Using either pins or an erasable pen, mark the outline of the card piece on the right side of the fabric cover to create an appliqué guideline.

3▶ Place each piece of fusing web, paper side up, on an appliqué motif. Trace the motif using a fairly dark pen. Following the manufacturer's instructions, fuse the web tracing to the wrong side of the appliqué fabric. Cut out the shape.

4▶ Position the appliqués on the right side of the cover, within the guideline. Remove the paper backing from each motif in turn, and fuse it to the fabric.

5▶ Glue the wadding piece to the card piece.

6▶ Lay the cover wrong side up, and centre the board, wadding side down, on top. Wrap all the edges of the fabric to the back of the board, and glue in place, pleating the fabric at the corners to fit.

7▶ Wrap the strip of piping fabric around the piping cord, with wrong sides facing and edges matching. Using the zipper foot on the sewing machine, stitch close to the cord.

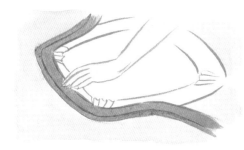

and the uncovered end of the cord so that they butt together. Turn under about 1.2cm (½in) on the edge of the overlapping fabric, and wrap the fabric around the join. Pin the ends together. (See Piped Bed Set pp. 84–85, for an illustration of this technique.)

9 ▶ Glue the covered card to the top of the picnic basket.

8 ▶ Glue the piping to the back of the card around the edges, so that the cord extends over the edge and the ends overlap slightly. Using a needle or sharp-pointed scissors, remove the stitches for approximately 4cm (1½in) from one end of the piping, and fold back the fabric. Trim the covered end

SILVER SERVER

Add beauty to a buffet dinner with a lace-trimmed silver server.

CHECKLIST

Materials

60cm (⅝yd) of 115cm (45in)-wide furnishing fabric
60cm (⅝yd) of 115cm (45in)-wide iron-on interfacing
1.9m (2yd) of 3cm (1¼in)-wide flat lace trimming
1 round lace doily, 25cm (10in) in diameter
50cm (½yd) of 1.5cm (⅝in)-wide ribbon
General sewing equipment
Paper for pattern

Techniques

Making patterns and cutting shapes	pp. 16–17
Machine stitching	pp. 22–23
Hand stitching	pp. 22–23
Applying trimmings	pp. 16–17

Making the pattern

Measure and cut a 8cm (20in)-diameter circle from the pattern paper.
Using a pencil and ruler, divide it into 12 equal segments.
Pattern size includes 1.2cm (½in) seam allowance.

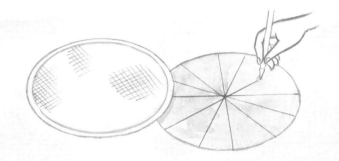

1 Use the pattern to cut two circles from the fabric and two from the interfacing. Trim 1.2cm (½in) seam allowance from the edge of the interfacing. Mark the edge of one fabric circle with the segment divisions from the pattern. Then use a ruler and erasable pen, on the right side, to link up these marks with straight lines. Following the instructions, fuse the interfacing to the wrong side of each circle.

2 Pin the lace trim to the right side of the marked circle, placing the straight edge just outside the seamline and the other edge towards the centre. Stitch the trim in place, overlapping ends to neaten them.

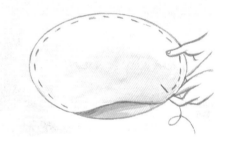

3 Pin and stitch the two circles together with the right sides together and the edges even, leaving a 15cm (6in) opening.

4 Trim the seam and clip the curves. Turn right side out through the opening. Slipstitch the opening closed. Press the server flat.

5 Pin the doily to the centre of the server. Sew the doily in place along the outside edge.

6 Fold the server in half and pin the edges together, taking care to match the segment markings. Stitch through all layers along the marked lines, securing the threads with a knot at each end. Erase the lines with water or just allow them to fade, depending on the type of pen.

7 Tie the ribbon in a bow and sew it to centre front of the doily.

For a greater number of place settings, cut the circle a few centimetres (inches) larger, and divide the sections accordingly, choosing an even number.

To make this project simpler, apply the heart-shaped doilies with fabric glue, and use pinking shears to give an attractive zigzag edge which needs no hemming.

MOCK AUSTRIAN BLIND PELMET

Only one seam is required to make this pretty pelmet, which imitates a raised Austrian blind.

C H E C K L I S T

Materials

Furnishing fabric
General sewing equipment
6cm (2½in)-wide flat curtain rod
Tissue paper

Techniques

Measuring up: windows	pp. 12–13
Installing window treatments	pp. 12–13
Joining fabric widths	pp. 14–15
Machine stitching	pp. 22–23

Measuring up

Measure the width of the window frame between its outside edges and the length down to the sill.

Cutting sizes

For the cutting length, divide the measured window length by 2; add 27cm (10½in).
For the cutting width, multiply the measured window width by 2½; add 10cm (4in).
If necessary piece several widths of fabric together to achieve the total width. The valance will have a 2½:1 fullness ratio and will cover approximately one-quarter of the window length.
Cutting sizes include 1.2cm (½in) seam allowance.

1 Turn under and press 5cm (2in) on the short side edges of the panel. Tuck the cut edge in to meet the fold and press again. Topstitch the double hem along the inside fold.

2 Using an erasable pen, mark a stitching line 9cm (3½in) from the top edge, on the right side of the fabric, and a fold line 13cm (5in) from this edge.

3 Placing right sides together and cut edges even, stitch the long edges of the panel together forming a long tube. Allow a 1.2cm (½in) seam. Press seam open. Turn pelmet right side out.

4 Pin pelmet layers together along previously marked fold line and press a crease. The seam and the marked stitching line are now on the back.

5 Pin layers together along seamline and stitching line. Stitch through all layers in the channel of the seamline and along marked stitching line to create the rod pocket.

6 To install the pelmet, slide it onto the rod distributing it evenly. Crumple several pieces of tissue paper and insert them into the pelmet to create the fullness.

FLAT CASED CURTAIN

The simplest of all window treatments shows off some fabric too beautiful to pleat or gather.

C H E C K L I S T

Materials

Furnishing fabric
Lining fabric
General sewing equipment
Liquid seam sealant
Paper-backed 1cm (⅜in)-wide fusing web strip
Two tension rods

Techniques

Measuring up: windows	pp. 12–13
Joining fabric widths	pp. 14–15
Fusing fabric	pp. 24–25

Measuring up

Measure the width and length of the window inside the window frame. Determine the finished length: between one-quarter and one-half the measured length of the window.

Making the pattern

Furnishing Fabric Panel For the cutting width, add 7.5cm (3in) to the width of the window. For the cutting length, add 10cm (4in) to the chosen finished length.
Lining Panel For the cutting width, add 2.5cm (1in) to the measured width. For the cutting length, add 5cm (2in) to the finished length. Piece several widths of fabric together, if necessary, to achieve the total width. Depending upon the window size, the cutting width may exceed the cutting length. Cutting sizes include 2.5cm (½in) seam allowance.

1 Using a liquid seam sealant, seal the upper and lower edges of the furnishing fabric.

2 Place the lining right side up. Apply a strip of fusing web to the seam allowance on both side edges.

3 Lay the furnishing fabric right side up, and place the lining on top, right side down, with two side edges even and an equal amount of the furnishing fabric showing at top and bottom. Fuse the lining to the furnishing fabric along this edge.

4 Move the lining over so that its other side edge meets that of the furnishing fabric. Fuse again.

5 Turn the curtain right side out. Press the curtain flat, allowing a 2.5cm (1in) facing of fabric to wrap to the wrong side of the curtain along each edge. Fuse the facing to the front of the curtain along the short edges above and below the lining.

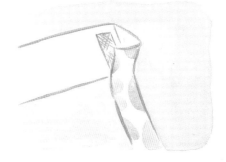

6 Apply a strip of fusing web to the wrong side of the furnishing fabric along the top and bottom seam allowances.

7 Turn under 5cm (2in) on the upper and lower edges of the curtain and pin these edges in place. Press the creases and then fuse these hems in place.

8 To install the curtain, slide two tension rods through the top and bottom hems, and mount the rods inside the window moulding. This will ensure the curtain is held taut between the rods.

PILLOWCASE CAFÉ CURTAINS

Much of the sewing is completed before you begin when you use pillowcases for café-style curtains.

CHECKLIST

Materials

Pillowcases
2 fabrics for appliqué
General sewing equipment
Paper-backed fusing web

Techniques

Measuring up windows	pp. 12–13
Installing window treatments	pp. 12–13
Cutting and joining widths	pp. 16–17
Machine stitching	pp. 22–23

Measuring up

Measure the width and length of the window frame's outside edge down to the sill.

Cutting sizes

Pelmet The cutting width should be twice the measured window width. The length should be one-quarter the measured length plus 7.5cm (3in).
Curtains The cutting width of each curtain should equal the measured window width. The length should be one-half the measured window length plus 7.5cm (3in).
Cut open the pillowcases along the manufacturer's seams, and piece several together, if necessary, to achieve the total width required. Use the top section only – the part with the decorative hem. The back and tuck-in sections can be saved for use in another project.
Sizes include 1.2cm (½in) seam allowances.

1 Measuring from the hemmed edge of the pillowcase, mark the cutting length of the pelmet and curtains. Measure and mark the width of the pelmet and curtains, making sure to mark at a right angle to the hem.

2 Turn under and press 5cm (2in) on the side edges of each panel. Tuck the cut edge in to meet the fold and press again. Topstitch the hem in place along the inside fold.

3 Turn under and press 1.2cm (½in) on the top edge of each panel. On the same edge, turn under 6cm (2½in) and press again. Pin this heading in place along the first fold.

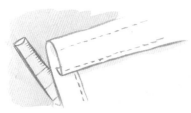

4 On all panels, stitch along the first, lower, fold. Measure and mark 3cm (1¼in) up from the first line of stitching and stitch along the marked line.

5 Decide on the number of appliqués needed. Apply enough fusing web to the wrong side of the appliqué fabric to accommodate the size and number of appliqués. Do not remove the paper backing. Using the patterns provided in the Templates section (pp. 120–25) and placing them on the wrong side of the fabric, mark the shapes; cut them out.

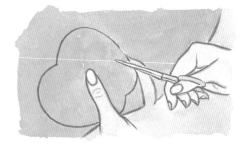

6 Position the appliqués on the hem of each piece; mark their positions lightly with a temporary marking pen. Remove the paper backing, and fuse the appliqué to the curtains and pelmet.

The decorative hem
of this pillowcase
provides the perfect
background for
simple fused
appliqués. See pages
120–5 for
templates. Instead
of making your own
appliqué motifs, you
could see what is
available
readymade.

ARMCHAIR COVER

Fabric is simply draped over an armchair for an easy-to-sew loose cover.

C H E C K L I S T

Materials

Furnishing fabric
Twisted furnishing cord
1.2cm (½in)-wide elastic or a drawstring
Metal eyelets to fit cord
General sewing equipment

Techniques

Joining fabric widths	pp. 14–15
Machine stitching	pp. 23–23
Hand stitching	pp. 22–23

Measuring up

Remove the seat cushion and measure its width, length and thickness. Measure the width of the chair from the floor at the side, over the shoulder, across the back and over the other shoulder down to the floor. Measure the length of the chair from the floor in front, across the seat and over the back down to the floor.

Cutting sizes

Cushion The cutting width equals the length of the cushion plus twice the thickness plus 15cm (6in). The cutting length equals the length of the cushion plus twice the thickness plus 15cm (6in).
Chair The cutting width is approximately 50cm (1½ft) greater than the measured width of the chair. Piece several fabric widths together, if necessary, to achieve cutting width. The cutting length is approximately 50cm (1½ft) greater than the measured length of the chair. Cutting sizes include 1.2cm (½in) hem allowance.

1 Following the cutting dimensions, cut one cushion cover and one chair cover.

2 Use a dinner plate as a template to round off all the corners of each fabric piece.

To complete the cushion cover:

3 This step is optional, depending on the type of chair. Turn under and press 5mm (¼in) on all edges of the cushion cover. Turn under edges again, this time 2cm (¾in), and press. Pin and stitch along the second fold, leaving a small opening to insert the elastic.

4 This step is also optional, depending on the type of armchair. Insert the elastic or a drawstring in the casing of the cushion cover. Place the cushion into the cover, draw the elastic tight and secure.

To complete the chair cover:

5 Turn under and press 1.2cm (½in) on all edges of the chair cover. Turn up 1.2cm (½in) again and press. Stitch close to the second fold.

6 Drape the cover over the chair, and arrange it so that the hem of the cover is even with the floor on all sides. Tuck the excess fabric into the gaps of the chair where the arms and back meet the deck of the seat to achieve this. If your cushion is removable, follow step 4 and replace to secure the cover.

▷ Measure the approximate depth from the bottom of the cushion to the floor. Collect the excess fabric at the four corners of the chair and hold the gathers together with a large safety pin.

Here, the cover has been further simplified by using a decorative kilt pin to gather up the fabric at the corners.

8 Mark the fabric where the gathering ends at each end of the safety pin. Remove the safety pin. Following the manufacturer's instructions, apply metal eyelets at the marks.

9 Cut a piece of furnishing cord about 1m (1yd) long for each corner of the chair. Slip the cord through the holes. Collect the excess fabric and tie a bow to secure. To prevent the cord ends from untwisting, tie a knot approximately 5cm (2in) from each end of the cord, then fluff out the ends.

FRILLED CHAIR CUSHION

Adding a foam block cushion covered with fabric to a straight-backed wooden chair makes sitting in it far more comfortable.

C H E C K L I S T

Materials

Furnishing fabric
5cm (2in)-thick polyurethane foam
1.4m (1½yd) grosgrain ribbon
General sewing equipment
Paper for pattern (optional)

Techniques

Machine stitching   pp. 22–23

Measuring up

Measure the width and length of the chair seat. If the seat is not a perfect rectangle, draw a paper pattern of the shape.

Cutting sizes

Foam block Add 5cm (2in) to the width of the chair seat and 2.5cm (1in) to the length; draw a rectangle to this size on the foam block. Or, if you have drawn a pattern of the seat, add 2.5cm (1in) to the front and side edges of this pattern, then cut out this enlarged pattern and draw around it on the foam. Either cut the foam with an electric carving knife or have it cut at a decorator's workroom.
Main piece Add 18cm (7in) to the width of the foam block and 9cm (3½in) to the depth. Or add 9cm (3½in) to the front and side edges of the enlarged pattern used to cut the block.
Frill The cutting width is 13cm (5in). For the cutting length, measure the side and front edges of the foam block and multiply by 2½. Piece fabric widths together if necessary to achieve this length.
Cutting sizes include 1.2cm (½in) seam allowance.

1 ▷ Following the cutting dimensions, cut one each of the main piece and frill. Use a saucer as a template to round off the corners of the main piece.

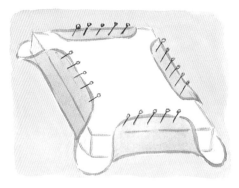

2 ▷ Lay the main piece on a flat surface, wrong side up, and place the foam block on top, centred. Fold the fabric edges over the foam and hold them in place with pins.

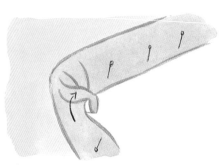

3 ▷ At each corner, form several small pleats in the fabric so that the fabric covers the foam neatly. Hand-tack the pleats in place. Remove the foam block.

4 ▷ Turn under and press 2.5cm (1in) on the short ends of the frill. Tuck the cut edges in to meet the folds and press again. Topstitch the double hems along the inner folds.

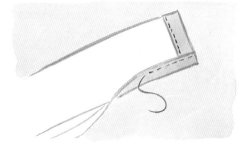

5 ▷ Hem one long edge of the frill, following the instructions in step 4.

6 ▷ Measure one side edge of the main cover piece, between the centre of the two pleated areas. Make a note of this measurement. Similarly, measure the front edge and note its measurement. Multiply each measurement by 2½. On the cut edge of the frill, mark off the enlarged side and front edge measurements. (You may need to adjust the marks slightly in order to make the side sections of the frill even).

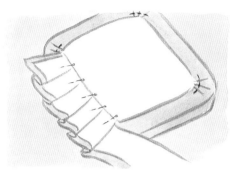
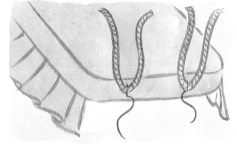

7 Placing right sides and cut edges together, pin the frill to one side edge of the main cover piece at two adjacent corners. Fold the fabric into seven or eight even pleats, and pin these in place. Repeat on the front edge and the other side edge.

8 Hand-tack the frill to the main cover, then stitch them together, press the seam flat and neaten the seam allowances. Insert the foam block in the cover.

9 Cut the grosgrain ribbon in half. Find the centre point of each piece, and sew this to the back edge of the cushion cover just behind the side struts of the chair, taking care not to sew into the foam. Tie the ribbons around the chair struts to hold the cushion in place. Trim the ribbon ends neatly.

The pleats of this frill neaten this easy-to-make cushion cover. For a softer look you could simply gather the frill.

LOOSE-COVERED SOFA

Cover a sofa with a large rectangle of fabric. Hold it in place with decorator cord or fringe.

CHECKLIST

Materials

Furnishing fabric
Twisted furnishing cord or heavy fringe
Large safety pins
General sewing equipment

Techniques

Joining fabric widths	pp. 14–15
Machine stitching	pp. 22–23

Measuring up

Measure the depth of the sofa from the floor in front, across the seat and over the back down to the floor.
Measure the length of the sofa from the floor at one side, up over the shoulder, across the back, over the other shoulder, and down to the floor.

Cutting sizes

The cutting width is approximately 50cm (1½ft) greater than the depth of the sofa. The cutting length is approximately 50cm (1½ft) greater than the length of the sofa. Piece several fabric widths together, if necessary, to achieve the cutting length. Cutting size includes 2.5cm (1in) hem allowance.

1 Following the cutting dimensions, cut one rectangle of fabric. Use a dinner plate as a template to round off the corners of the cover.

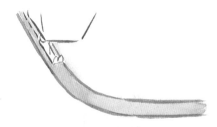

2 Turn under and press 1.2cm (½in) on all edges. Turn under another 1.2cm (½in) and press. Stitch close to the second fold.

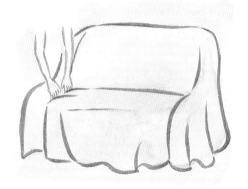

3 Drape the cover over the sofa. Tuck the excess fabric into the gaps where the arms and back meet the seat cushions, until the hem of the cover is even with the floor on all sides. Alternatively, tuck some fabric into the gaps and allow the excess to flow onto the floor on all sides of the sofa.

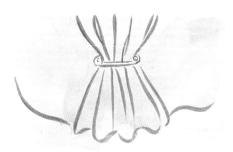

4 Measure the approximate depth from the bottom of the cushions to the floor. Collect the excess fabric at the four corners of the sofa and hold the gathers together with a large safety pin at this level.

5 Wrap a length of heavy twisted furnishing cord or very wide bullion fringe around the base of the sofa. Join the ends of the trimming together at the back with safety pins. Secure it to the fabric at random points with more safety pins, hidden from view.

The hem of the cover is made even with the floor by tucking the excess fabric into the gaps of the sofa where the arms and back meet the seat cushion. Use fusing web to hem the fabric for a no-sew alternative.

SPLENDID SEATS

As a clever alternative to time-consuming tailored loose covers, cover your sofa or chairs with wrap and tie casual loose covers. To protect the upholstery underneath, choose durable fabric and a dark colour – perfect for families with young children. To make a holiday party more festive, make something new for your sofa to wear. Or for a welcome change of pace, choose a pastel print for the warm summer months and a cosy check for the winter. These covers are so simple and appealing, you will want to make several.

Tied seat cover
Bring your old chair to life with an easy-to-make tied seat cover. Cut enough material so that it hangs over the edge, remove excess material at the corners and attach ribbon or furnishing cord to hold the cover in place. This is so quick and easy that it can be used as a permanent cover or to temporarily change the appearance of a room for a special occasion.

Covered pouffe
Give an old pouffe a facelift with a generous draping of fabric and attractively knotted cords.

Frilled armchair cover

A rich, dramatic colour was chosen for this ruched chair cover. A long strip of the fabric was used to cover the chair from the bottom front, over the cushion and the top, and down the back. For a temporary cover, secure it with safety pins, or stitch in place for a long-term furnishing change. The arms are made from separate pieces of material. At the top of the arm, sew a couple of rows of long, irregular running stitches. Pull on the threads to gather the fabric and tie off. Tuck one side of the fabric beneath the cushion and allow the rest to flow onto the floor.

Stool

Try this no sew, no fuss method of covering a child's stool. Glue foam to the stool top, then place wadding and fabric on top. Turn stool upside down and ensure that it is centred on the fabric. Gently pull fabric taut and, using a staple gun, attach to the underside of the stool.

AUSTRIAN BLIND

A slightly more ambitious project, this Austrian blind is inspired by designs from Victorian times.

C H E C K L I S T

Materials

Furnishing fabric
Paper-backed 1.5cm (⅝in)-wide fusing web strip
Austrian blind tape
2-cord gathered heading tape
Nylon cord
Decorative fringe
Mounting board and hardware
Thin metal rod
Large screw eyes
General sewing equipment

Techniques

Measuring up: windows	pp. 12–13
Installing window treatments	pp. 12–13
Joining fabric widths	pp. 14–15
Fusing fabric	pp. 24–25
Applying trimmings	pp. 16–17

Measuring up

Measure the window frame between its outside edges and from the mounting board position to the sill.

Cutting sizes

Blind To establish the cutting width, multiply the measured width of the window by 2. For the cutting length, multiply the measured length of the window by 1⅓.
Piece several widths of fabric together, if necessary, to achieve the total width.
The blind will have a 2 : 1 fullness ratio.
Rod cover The cutting length is the length of the metal rod plus 4cm (1½in). The width is the circumference of the rod plus 3cm (1¼in).

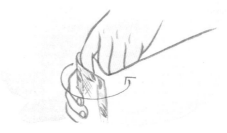

1 Turn under and press 5cm (2in) on each side edge. Tuck the edge in to meet the fold and press again. Open out the second fold. Apply fusing web to the hem along the folded edge. Remove the paper backing, refold the hem, and fuse in place.

2 Measuring from the folded edges, divide the blind width into equal thirds and mark these divisions on the wrong side. The distance between the marks should be not less than 30cm (12in). For wider windows, mark out more divisions; reduce the number for smaller windows.

3 Trim one end of the blind tape, so that the first ring is 4cm (1½in) from the cut edge. Measuring from this cut, leading edge, cut a length of ring tape equal to the cutting length of the blind.

Note: If the rings are too close to the edge to press the hem, carefully remove the stitches and discard the rings.

4 Cut three more pieces of blind tape, identical to the first.

5 Position each length of blind tape on the wrong side of the blind, along the side hems and marked lines, with the leading edge at the bottom. Pin the tape to the blind with the first ring positioned 6cm (2½in) from the lower edge of the blind.

6 Continue pinning each tape to the blind, keeping the tapes parallel and the rings directly opposite each other. Trim the tapes 2.5cm (1in) below the upper edge of the blind. Carefully stitch the tape to the side hems and marked lines.

7 Turn under and press 2.5cm (1in) on the upper edge. Following the manufacturer's instructions, apply fusing web to the hem along the folded edge. Remove the paper backing, refold the hem, and fuse in place, covering the cut edge of the blind tape.

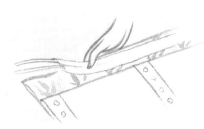

Easy-to-use curtain heading tape and Austrian blind tape create both the crosswise and lengthwise fullness and simplify the construction of this lavish Austrian blind.

8 Cut a length of heading tape equal to the width of the blind. Apply the tape to the upper edge of the blind between the side hems.

9 Turn under and press 5cm (2in) on the lower edge. Tuck the edge in to meet the fold, and press again.

10 Open out the second fold. Following the manufacturer's instructions, apply fusing web to this hem.

11 Stitch or fuse one or two rows of tassel fringe to the lower edge of the shade, turning under the ends to neaten them.

12 Fold the rod cover in half lengthwise, with right sides facing. Stitch the long edges together and across one end. Trim seam allowances, and, with the help of a knitting needle, turn right side out.

13 Slip the cover over the metal rod. Trim the end if necessary, turn it under, and sew it closed. Sew the rod in place at the lower edge of the blind, just under each ring, with a few hand stitches through the fabric.

14 Cut a length of cord for each length of blind tape, each measuring twice the length of the blind plus the width. Tie each cord securely to a bottom ring and thread it up through all the other rings.

15 Attach a screw eye to the mounting board at the position of each blind tape. Draw up the gathering tape at the top of the blind, and adjust the gathers evenly. Mount the blind on the board. Thread each cord through a screw eye and take all to one side of the window. With the blind down, tie the cords in a knot. Trim ends as necessary.

FRINGED CURTAIN

For a striking curtain, trim a single panel of fabric with heavy bullion fringe and hang it from a decorative pole.

CHECKLIST

Materials

Heavyweight furnishing fabric
15cm (6in) bullion fringe
1cm (⅜in)-wide ribbon
General sewing equipment
Fabric glue

Techniques

Measuring up: windows	pp. 12–13
Installing window treatments	pp. 12–13
Joining fabric widths	pp. 14–15
Machine stitching	pp. 22–23
Hand stitching	pp. 22–23

Measuring up

Measure the width of the window frame between its outside edges. Measure the length from the pole to the floor.

Cutting sizes

Curtain Panel For the cutting width, multiply the window width by 2. For the cutting length, subtract the width of the fringe from the window length, then add 8cm (3in).
Tieback Cut one rectangle 23cm x 74cm (9in x 29in).
Piece several widths of fabric together if necessary to achieve the total curtain width. The curtain will have a 2:1 fullness ratio, and the lower edge of the fringe will hang 1.2cm (½in) above the floor. If you want the drapery to flow on to the floor, add 38cm (15in). The cutting measurements allow for a 4cm (1½in)-deep casing pole. Increase the cutting length for a thicker pole.

1 Turn under and press 2.5cm (1in) on the lower edge. Tuck the cut edge in to meet the fold and press again. Stitch along the second fold.

2 Turn under and press 2.5cm (1in) on each side edge. Tuck the cut edge in to meet the fold and press again. Stitch along the second fold.

3 On the right side of the fabric, stitch or glue the heading of the fringe to the hems of the curtain, so that the fringe itself extends past the curtain hem. Begin and end at the cut upper edge of the curtain, and mitre the corners at the lower edge.

4 Turn under and press 1.2cm (½in) on the upper edge of the drape. Turn under and press a further 4cm (1½in). Insert the decorative pole in the casing to double check this measurement. Adjust the width, if necessary, and remove the pole. Stitch along the first fold.

To make the tieback:

5 Fold the rectangle in half lengthwise with right sides facing. Stitch together both short ends and the one long edge, leaving a small opening for turning.

▶ Turn the fabric right side out, and slipstitch the opening edges together. Press the tieback flat.

▶ On one side, sew or glue the heading of the fringe to the lower and side edges of the tieback. Begin and end at the upper edge of the curtain, turning under the end of the fringe. Mitre the corners at the lower edge.

▶ Cut two 8cm (3in) pieces of ribbon. Make each into a small loop and sew to the upper corners of the tieback.

Gluing the decorative fringe in place eliminates the task of sewing through a heavy trimming.

FUSED AND PLEATED CURTAINS

Making this classic curtain style is simplified by the use of fused hems and pleat tape.

C H E C K L I S T

Materials

Decorator fabric
Paper-backed 1.5cm (⅝in)-wide fusing web strip
Fusible French pleat tape
General sewing equipment

Techniques

Measuring up: windows	pp. 12–13
Installing window treatments	pp. 12–13
Joining fabric widths	pp. 14–15
Machine stitching	pp. 22–23
Fusing fabric	pp. 24–25

Measuring up

Measure the length of the window from the rod to the floor.

Cutting sizes

Because calculating the cutting size of the curtains takes some time, the information you need to do it is given in the main project instructions, steps 1–5.
Cutting sizes include 1.2cm (½in) seam allowance.

1 ▶ The pleated width of the curtain will equal the measured length of the mounted pole plus two returns to the wall. For each curtain, divide this distance by 2 and add the centre overlap – about 5cm (2in).

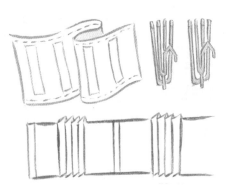

2 ▶ The cutting dimensions are determined by the window width and the spacing between pockets on the type of pleat tape purchased. The cutting width of each curtain measures approximately three times the finished width. For an exact measurement, first insert pleat hooks in the curtain tape, leaving the required spacing between pleats.

3 ▶ Hook the pleat tape to the pole with the first pleat positioned at the outside corner. Allow the tape to lie flat in the return area from the front corner of the pole to the wall and in the centre overlap area between the two panels. Mark the tape at the wall and the front end.

4 ▶ Measure the finished length of the curtains from the top of the pleat tape to the floor, and mark the measurement.

5 ▶ Remove the tape from the pole and the hooks from the tape. Add 1.2cm (½in) to the marks you have just made. This gives you the cutting length of the pleat tape.

The cutting width of each panel is equal to the finished length of the pleat tape, plus 20cm (8in) for side hems. For the cutting length of each panel, take the measured length and add twice the width of the pleat tape plus 20cm (8in) for the lower hem.

Piece two or more widths of fabric together, if necessary, to achieve the total curtain width. The curtain panels should be exactly the same size.

6▶ Following the cutting dimensions, cut two panels.

To make one panel:

7▶ Turn under and press 20cm (8in) on the lower edge. Tuck the cut edge in to meet the fold and press again.

8▶ Open out the second fold. Following the manufacturer's instructions, apply fusing web to the hem along the folded edge. Remove the paper backing, refold the hem, and fuse in place.

9▶ To hem the side edges of the curtain, repeat steps 7 and 8 making an initial fold of 10cm (4in), rather than 20cm (8in).

10▶ On the upper edge, turn under twice the width of the pleat tape; press. Tuck the cut edge in to meet the fold and press again.

11▶ Open out the second fold. Following the manufacturer's instructions, apply fusing web to the hem along the folded edge. Remove the paper backing, refold the hem, and fuse in place.

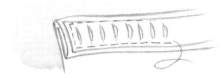

12▶ Pin the pleat tape to the centre of the upper hem. Turn under the ends to neaten, and stitch through all layers on all edges of the tape.

13▶ Leaving the returns flat, insert the hooks in the tape. Hang the curtains from the pole.

These curtains look difficult to make, but the relatively simple measuring method and the use of pleat tape mean that even someone without much sewing experience can make them successfully.

SPIRALLING TASSELS

A centre swag and spiralling tails make an unusual window treatment.

C H E C K L I S T

Materials

Furnishing fabric
Tassel braid
Fusible gathered heading tape
Hook and loop tape
General sewing equipment
Mounting board and hardware

Techniques

Measuring windows	pp. 12–13
Installing window treatments	pp. 12–13
Fusing fabric	pp. 24–25
Machine stitching	pp. 22–23

Measuring up

Measure the width of the window frame between the outside edges and the length to the floor. Use a cord to determine the length of the swag. Fasten one end to the wall or window frame at the chosen position for the lower edge after gathering, then drape the cord down and up to the corresponding point on the other side. Measure the cord.

Cutting sizes

Swag The cutting width is 46cm (18in). The cutting length is equal to the measured swag length plus 2.5cm (1in).
Tails The cutting width is 46cm (18in). For the cutting length, double the measured window length.
Cutting sizes include 1.2cm (½in) hem allowance.

1 Following the cutting dimensions, cut one swag and two tails. Add 2.5cm (1in) to the measured window width; record this measurement and mark it off in the centre of one long edge of the swag rectangle. Draw a straight line from the marks to the adjacent corners, and trim the ends to create the swag shape.

2 Neaten all the cut edges on all the pieces.

3 Turn under and press 1.2cm (½in) on all the edges of all the pieces. Stitch 1cm (⅜in) from folded edge.

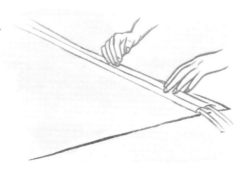

4 Following the manufacturer's instructions, apply the heading tape to each angled side edge of the swag on the wrong side of the fabric. Do not pull the cords yet.

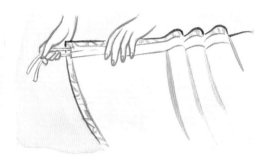

5 Apply the heading tape to the other long edge of each tail on the wrong side of the fabric. Pull the heading tape cords to gather the fabric.

6 Stitch the tassel braid to the inner long edge of each tail (the edge that will hang nearer the centre) and to the lower edge, on the right side of the fabric.

7 Because heading tapes gather at different rates, check the length of the tail by temporarily attaching it to the mounting board. Pull the heading tape cords and allow the tail to spiral towards the floor. Adjust the gathers until the gathered edge is hidden by the hemmed edge on each spiral.

Trim the fabric to adjust the length if necessary. Remove the fabric from the board. Secure the cords by knotting at both ends.

10 ▶ Staple or glue the hook (stiff) half of the tape to the top of the mounting board at the edge closest to the wall.

8 On the right side of the fabric, stitch the tassel braid to the two short edges and lower long edge of the swag. Pull the heading tape cords to gather the fabric. Secure the cord ends by knotting them.

11 Staple the top edge of each tail to the top of the mounting board at the side. Position the swag over the tails on the installed mounting board by joining the hook and loop tapes.

9 ▶ Cut the hook and loop tape to equal the window width. Stitch the loop (fuzzy) half of the tape to the wrong side of the swag, on the untrimmed edge.

The swag and tails can be used with matching floor-length curtains, as shown, or hung by themselves over shutters or a Venetian blind.

To make the no-sew version, use a liquid seam sealant to neaten the edges, fusing web tape for the hems, and fabric glue to apply the tassel braid.

ZIGZAG PELMET

A casing is not needed for this pelmet, since the weight of the fabric holds it in place.

CHECKLIST

Materials

Furnishing fabric
Braid trimming and tassels
General sewing equipment
Paper for pattern

Techniques

Making patterns	pp. 16–17
Machine stitching	pp. 22–23

Measuring up

Measure the the length of the mounted pole. Measure the length of the window from the pole to the sill. The pelmet will be two-thirds this length, so that, when hung, it will cover one-third of the window.

Cutting sizes

Pelmet and *Lining* For the cutting width, add 2.5cm (1in) to the measured length of the pole. For the cutting length, add 2.5cm (1in) to the finished length.
Piece several fabric widths together, if necessary, to achieve the cutting width.
Cutting sizes include 1.2cm (½in) seam

1 For best results, make a paper pattern, following the instructions given in steps 2–7, and mount the pattern on the pole to check its proportions before cutting the fabrics.

2 Following the cutting dimensions, cut the basic rectangle.

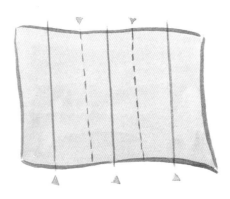

3 For the distance between points, divide the finished width of the pelmet by 3. For a very wide window, divide by a greater number. Mark this distance the appropriate number of times at the top edge of the pattern. Mark the same distance along the bottom edge, but split the measurement at the two sides.

4 Find the horizontal centre of the pelmet. Mark two lines across the centre of the pelmet 15cm (6in) apart.

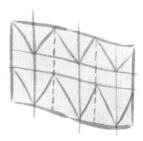

5 On the lower of these lines, mark the previously determined distance between points. On the upper line, mark the distance, but split the measurement at the two sides.

6 Matching the marks, draw three whole points at the lower edge and two whole and two half points at the upper edge.

7 Cut the pattern along the diagonal lines, trimming away the upper and lower triangles.

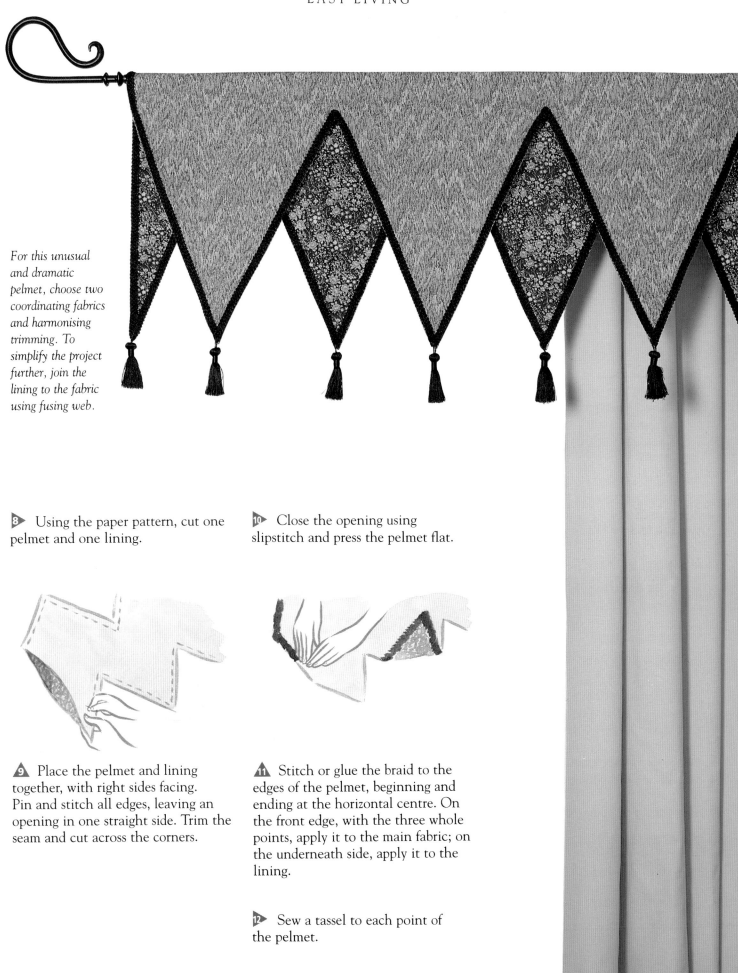

For this unusual and dramatic pelmet, choose two coordinating fabrics and harmonising trimming. To simplify the project further, join the lining to the fabric using fusing web.

8 ▶ Using the paper pattern, cut one pelmet and one lining.

10 ▶ Close the opening using slipstitch and press the pelmet flat.

9 ▶ Place the pelmet and lining together, with right sides facing. Pin and stitch all edges, leaving an opening in one straight side. Trim the seam and cut across the corners.

11 ▶ Stitch or glue the braid to the edges of the pelmet, beginning and ending at the horizontal centre. On the front edge, with the three whole points, apply it to the main fabric; on the underneath side, apply it to the lining.

12 ▶ Sew a tassel to each point of the pelmet.

ROD POCKET PELMET

This easy-to-make pelmet slips over an extra-wide curtain rod attached to a fabric-covered pelmet board.

CHECKLIST

Materials

Printed furnishing fabric
Plain furnishing fabric
General sewing equipment
11cm (4½in)-wide flat curtain rod

Techniques

Measuring up: windows	pp. 12–13
Installing window treatments	pp. 12–13
Joining fabric widths	pp. 14–15
Machine stitching	pp. 22–23

Measuring up

Measure the window frame between its outside edges.

Making the pattern

Rod Sleeve and Headings The cutting width is 15cm (6in). For the cutting length, multiply the measured window width by 3.
Back Facing The cutting width is 41cm (16in). For the cutting length, multiply the measured window width by 3.
Piece several widths of fabric together if necessary, to achieve cutting lengths.
Cutting sizes include 1.2cm (½in) seam

1 Following the cutting dimensions, cut one rod sleeve from plain fabric. Cut two headings and one facing from printed fabric.

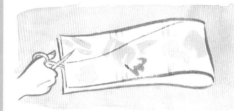

2 On one heading, measure 7.5cm (3in) up from one long edge on a short edge; mark this point. Fold the heading in half crosswise, and mark the other long edge 7.5cm (3in) in from the fold. Draw a tapered line between the marks. Cut along the line through both layers. Save one trimmed-off piece for use later.

3 Open the folded heading. Using the trimmed heading as a pattern, cut the other heading the same shape. If you are using a directional fabric, the shaping should be applied to the lower edge on the second heading.

4 Using the trimmed-off piece from step 2 as a pattern, shape the upper and lower edges of the facing.

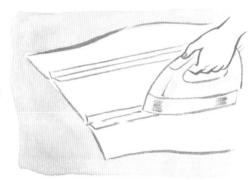

5 Placing right sides and long straight edges together, stitch the headings to the rod pocket. Press the seams open.

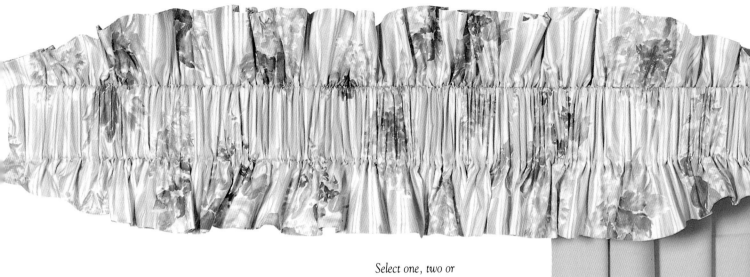

Select one, two or three coordinating fabrics for this easy-to-sew pelmet.

As an alternative to hemming the ends with stitching use strips of fusing web.

8 ▶ With right sides facing, stitch the front assembly to the facing along the upper and lower edges. Trim the seam allowances, clip the curves, and press the seams open.

9 ▶ Turn the pelmet right side out and press flat. Pin the layers together along the rod pocket and heading seams. Stitch through all the layers in the ditch of the seams, backstitching and tying threads securely at the ends.

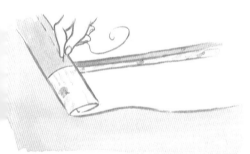

6 ▶ Turn under and press 5cm (2in) on one short end of the heading-sleeve assembly. Tuck the cut edge in to meet the fold and press again. Topstitch the double hem along the inside fold. Repeat for the opposite short end.

7 ▶ Repeat step 6 on the facing.

WINNING WINDOWS

Whether you wish to make a grand statement with one graceful sweep of fabric or just add a touch of colour with a small frilled pelmet, you can choose from one of the many sewing and fusing techniques shown here to create an interesting window treatment. Follow easy measuring techniques for making simple rectangles and circles to create clever curtains and blinds for any size window. Frame the view, control the light and increase your privacy with a few carefully placed seams and hems.

Draped swag
Disguised as an intricate custom-made swag, this simple-to-make draped swag is created using long rectangles of fabric and lace. Fold the fabrics into wide concertina-style pleats before draping it over a decorative brass pole. For very long swags, pin the folds together with extra large safety pins until the fabric is on the pole and ready to be arranged.

Roman blind
Attractive and easy-to-make, the Roman blind could be the perfect choice for many of the rooms in your home. The use of fusing web for the hemming and ring tape for the gathering makes this sophisticated window treatment both simple and satisfying to complete.

Stagecoach blind
The stagecoach blind, as the name suggests, resembles the window coverings used in old-fashioned stagecoaches. Cut two coordinating fabrics to the inside width of the window and rather longer than the depth, allowing a little extra for seams. With right sides facing, sew them together, turn right side out, close and press. Staple the blind to a thick dowel and hang. The blind is rolled up by hand and held in place with matching fabric ties.

Tea towel café curtains
Teatowels used as the fabric for a simple window treatment make a truly coordinated kitchen. Follow the instructions for making the Pillowcase café curtains on page 42. You could create an attractive fringed edge to your curtains by cutting off the hem and fraying a little of the fabric. Depending on the size of your curtains, it may be better to use a different loosely-woven fabric rather than tea towels.

Mock Austrian blind pelmet
For the instructions for how to make this original window treatment, see page 40.

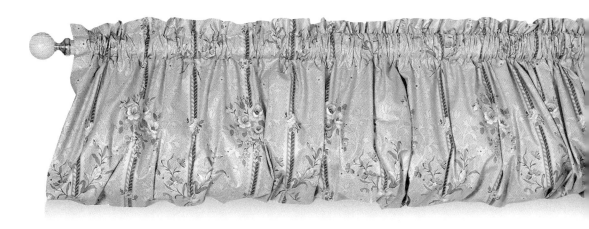

FABRIC SCREEN

Refurbish an old screen or decorate a new one with some fabric and painted floral motifs.

CHECKLIST

Materials

Wooden room divider screen
Furnishing fabric
1cm (³⁄₈in)-wide fusing web strip
General sewing equipment
Acrylic paint and brushes
Varnish

Techniques

Machine stitching	pp. 22–23
Fusing fabric	pp. 24–25

Measuring up

Measure the width of the screen opening. Measure the length of the opening from the front of the screen, over the upper dowel, around the lower dowel and up to the front again.

Cutting sizes

For the cutting width of the fabric, multiply the measured width of the opening by 2. For the cutting length of the fabric, take the total measured length and add twice the depth of the gathered heading plus 2.5cm (1in). The fabric will have a 2:1 fullness ratio. Multiply cutting sizes by the number of panels in the screen.
Cutting sizes include 1.2cm (½in) seam

1 If you are using a new screen, assemble it up to the point of attaching the hinges. Prepare the wood and apply a base coat of paint

2 Transfer your own design to the top of the screen (or see the Template section on pp. 120–25). You may need to enlarge or reduce the size of the flowers using a photocopier. By cutting apart sections of the design, you can alter the length or change the shape of the curve.

3 Using contrasting colours, paint the details of the design. Allow to dry thoroughly. Apply varnish and complete the screen assembly.

to the screen. Allow to dry, and if necessary apply a second coat. If you are using an old screen, remove the hardware and hinges.

To make one fabric panel:

4 Following the manufacturer's instructions, apply fusing web to the wrong side of the fabric on each long side edge of each fabric panel.

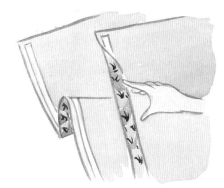

5 Turn under 2.5cm (1in) on both long side edges of the fabric panel; fuse the hems in place.

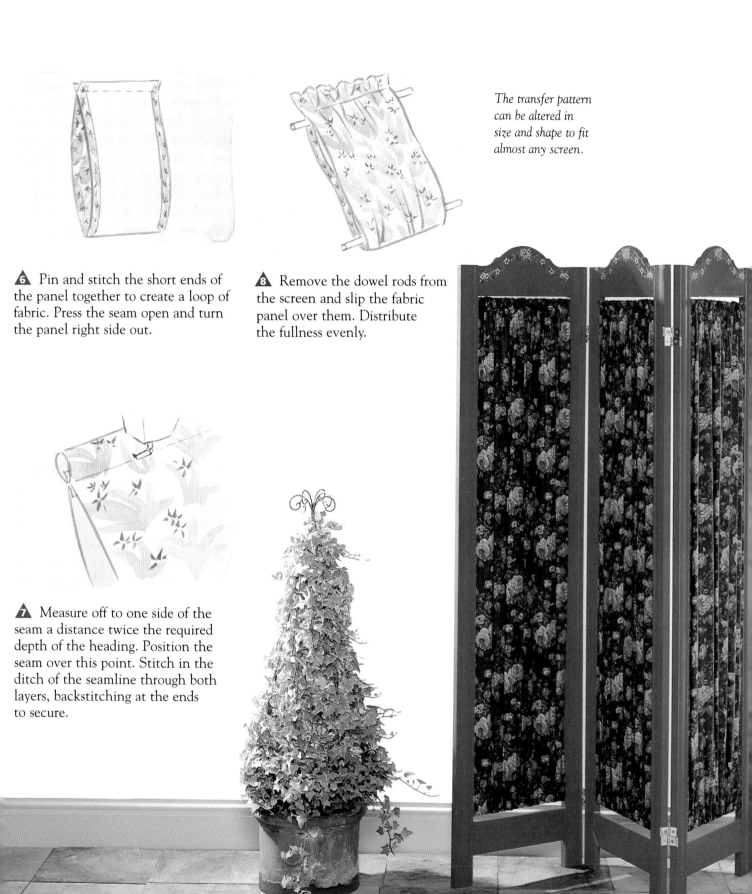

The transfer pattern can be altered in size and shape to fit almost any screen.

6 Pin and stitch the short ends of the panel together to create a loop of fabric. Press the seam open and turn the panel right side out.

8 Remove the dowel rods from the screen and slip the fabric panel over them. Distribute the fullness evenly.

7 Measure off to one side of the seam a distance twice the required depth of the heading. Position the seam over this point. Stitch in the ditch of the seamline through both layers, backstitching at the ends to secure.

SEW-FREE LAMPSHADES

Fusible curtain heading tape applied to one or both edges creates the gathers on these clever covers.

CHECKLIST

Materials

Conical lampshade
Furnishing or eyelet fabric
Fusible curtain heading tape
Fusing web strip
Ribbon or trimming
Fabric glue

Techniques

Fusing fabric   pp. 24–25

Measuring up

Measure the circumference of the lampshade at the narrower upper edge only. Measure the height of the lampshade from edge to edge. Note: This cover is not suitable for conical shades on which the circumference of the lower edge is more than 3 times that of the upper edge.

Cutting sizes

Shirred Lampshade For the cutting width, add 2.5cm (1in) to the height of the shade.
Hemmed Lampshade For the cutting width, add 7.5cm (3in) to the height of the shade.
Eyelet Lampshade For the cutting width, add 1.2cm (½in) to the height of the shade. Measure and cut the fabric to include the scalloped edge.
All lampshades For the cutting length, multiply the measured circumference by 3.

1▶ Turn under and press 1.2cm (½in) on the long upper edge of the lampshade cover.

2▶ Treat the lower edge of the cover in the following manner for each style of shade:

• For the Shirred Lampshade, turn under and press 1.2cm (½in).

• For the Hemmed Lampshade, turn under and press 5cm (2in). Tuck the cut edge in to meet the fold and press again. Apply fusing web to the inside of the hem, and fuse in place.

• For the Eyelet Lampshade, no finishing is required at the lower edge.

3 On one short edge of the cover turn under and press 1.2cm (½in). Apply a strip of fusing web to the seam allowance.

4 Place the cut short edges together, and fuse the seam, creating a cylindrical shape.

5 • For the Shirred Lampshade, cut two lengths of heading tape equal to the distance around the cover.
• For the Hemmed and the Eyelet Lampshades, cut one length of heading tape equal to the circumference of the cover. Beginning and ending at the seam, apply the tape either to the top edge, or to both edges of the cover on the wrong side, 5mm (¼in) from the fold.

6 Pull the cords of the tape to fit one or both edges of the lampshade, depending on the style, distributing the gathers evenly. Secure the cords with a knot, and trim excess cord. Glue the cover to the shade at one or both edges.

Note: For easy removal of the cover, use very little glue, applying it in small dabs at the upper edge only.

7 Glue a bow or some braid trimming to the top edge of the cover.

These no-sew lampshade covers allow you to transform a lamp either permanently or just temporarily — for a summery look, perhaps.

NO-SEW CUSHIONS

No sewing is required to make these cushions. Each can be made from items found in haberdashery and soft furnishing departments.

C H E C K L I S T

Materials

Square and bolster cushion pads
Scarves, napkins, pillowcases and/or fabric
Ribbon or trimming
Safety pins or elastic bands
General sewing equipment
Fabric glue

Measuring up

Measure the width and length of the square cushion pad. Measure the length of the bolster pad.
The pillowcase bolster uses an American-style pillowcase, which has no flap and on which the decorative edging, if any, goes all the way around the pillow. If you cannot find this kind of pillowcase, you could substitute a single bed sheet.

For the pillow case bolster

1 Purchase one pillowcase with a decorative hem and a small bolster cushion pad. You will also need 4 elastic bands, 2m (6ft) of ribbon and 5 ribbon roses.

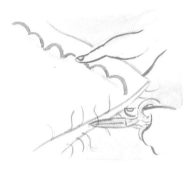

2 Cut open the pillowcase along the long and short seams. Do not un-stitch the hem. Press flat.

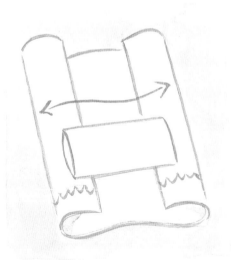

3 Turn under the long edges of the case, which run perpendicular to the hem, so that the distance between the folds is 25cm (10in) greater than the length of the bolster pad. Press the folds.

4 Beginning at the cut end, opposite the hem, roll the pillowcase around the pad. Gather up the pillowcase at both ends of the pad and wrap with elastic bands. Tie a ribbon around both ends, finishing with a bow. Glue ribbon roses along the hemline.

For the lace scarf cushion

1 Purchase one lace runner no wider than the chosen square cushion pad and 2–3 times its size in length. Cut a square of fabric 2½ times the size of the pad. You will also need 6 small safety pins and 1m (3ft) of ribbon.

2 Place the fabric wrong side up and lay the cushion pad in the centre. In the same way as you would cover a gift box, fold opposite ends of the fabric around the pad and pin in place.

3 Now fold the opposite ends of the fabric around the pad and pin in place. On the last fold, hide the pins under the fabric.

4 Place the covered cushion pad on the centre of the lace runner. Wrap the scarf ends to the right side of the pad and fold back any excess. Thread the ends of the ribbon through the lace holes on both sides of the runner. Tie the ribbon into a bow.

To make this pillowcase bolster, a pillowcase wrapped around a bolster pad is trimmed with ribbon roses and satin ribbons.

The attractive lace scarf cushion is made using fabric and a lace runner. They cover a square cushion pad and are secured with safety pins and a ribbon bow.

LOW-SEW CUSHIONS

Very few seams are needed to make these simple cushions. Twisted furnishing cord and buttons add the finishing touch.

CHECKLIST

Materials

Square and rectangular cushion pad
Furnishing fabrics
Buttons and cord
General sewing equipment

Techniques

Machine stitching   pp. 22–23

Measuring up

Measure the width and length of the cushion.

Cutting sizes

Tied Bag Cushion
For the cutting width, multiply the width/length of the square cushion pad by 2 and add 2.5cm (1in). For the length, multiply by 2½.
Button Cushion
Centre For the cutting width, add 2.5cm (1in) to the width of the cushion pad. For the cutting length, multiply the length of the pad by 2 and add 2.5cm (1in).
Borders The cutting width is 18cm (7in). For the cutting length, multiply the length of the pad by 2 and add 2.5cm (1in).
Cutting sizes include 1.2cm (½in) seam allowance.

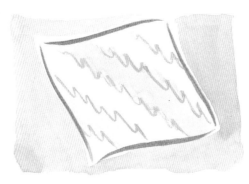

1▶ Following the cutting dimensions, cut one cover from furnishing fabric.

2▶ Fold the cover in half lengthwise with right sides facing. Pin and stitch the long side edge and the lower end of the cover. Neaten the seams and press them open.

3▶ Measuring from the lower seam, mark the size of the cushion pad on the seamed and folded edges. Fold down the cut edge at the open end to meet these marks. Press the fold.

4▶ Turn the cover right side out. Insert the pad and tie the opening closed with decorative cord, wrapping the cord several times around the opening.

To make the button cushion:

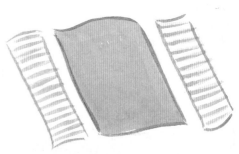

1▶ Following the cutting dimensions, cut one centre from furnishing fabric and two borders from a coordinating fabric.

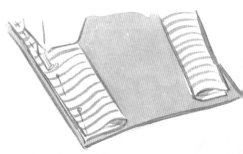

2▶ Fold the borders in half lengthwise with wrong sides together; press. Place the centre piece right side up, and pin the borders to its long edges with all raw edges matching; stitch. Neaten the seams and press towards the centre.

5 Insert the cushion pad. Holding the folded edges even, pin the borders together at each of the marks. Sew the buttons at the marks.

3 Fold the cover in half crosswise with right sides facing, matching the seams. Pin and stitch the remaining seam. Neaten the seam and press open. With the seam positioned at the lower edge, press the cushion cover flat.

Two seams are all that is needed to make this tied bag cushion.

As the name suggests, the button cushion is fastened with large buttons. These also help to set off the two coordinating fabrics.

4 Divide the finished flat width of the cover by 4 to get the spacing between the buttons. Mark the positions for the buttons along the centre of each border, allowing the full measurement between the buttons and half the measurement at each end.

CLEVER CUSHIONS

Add sparkle and interest to any room with easy-to-make scatter cushions. Carefully chosen colours and textures help to carry the eye around the room and unify the space creating the look of a professionally decorated room. Coordinate the entire room by using furnishing fabric left over from the window treatment or choose a contrasting fabric to introduce an additional colour. Cushions and accessories require little fabric, which makes them a perfect choice for luxurious and elegant fabrics which may be too costly to use for larger projects. For an interesting change of pace, try the cushion projects that substitute bed sheets and table linens for furnishing fabric.

Scarf cushion
This simple no-sew cushion was made using two attractive floral scarves held together on each side of the cushion pad with coordinating furnishing cord.

Fringed napkin cushion
Take two check napkins that are slightly larger than the cushion pad and tie them together at the corners.

pillow talk
Try a more dramatic style using contrasting coloured fabrics, as pictured here. The impact is increased by using generous amounts of luxurious fabric.

Cracker-style cushion
This attractive cushion is simple to produce. Hem your fabric with fusing web, then roll it around the bolster and secure the ends using coordinating ribbon.

73

DESK ACCESSORIES

This handy desk blotter and file folder will give a touch of class to a desk or home office.

CHECKLIST

Materials

Furnishing fabric
Multi-pocket file folder
2m (2yd) 2.5cm (1in)-wide ribbon
Thin and thick card
Lightweight wadding
Paper-backed fusing web and fabric glue
Scalpel or craft knife
Paper blotter

Techniques

Cutting shapes	pp. 16–17
Fusing fabric	pp. 24–25

Measuring up

Measure the paper blotter and the file holder (front and back) in both directions.

Cutting sizes

Desk Blotter
Base Cut the card equal in width and 10cm (4in) longer than the paper blotter.
Base Fabric and Fusing Web Cut 10cm (4in) wider and longer than the base.
Sides, Wadding Cut the length equal to the width of base; cutting width is 10cm (4in).
Side, Fabric Cut 10cm (4in) wider and longer than the sides.
File Folder
Card Front and Back Cut to the size of the front and back of the file folder.
Wadding Cut the wadding the same size as the back of the file folder.
Fabric Front and Back Cut each front and back piece 10cm (4in) wider and longer than the card pieces.

1 ▶ Following the cutting dimensions, use the scalpel to cut two base pieces and side pieces from thick card. Cut one base from fusing web and two side pieces from wadding.

2 ▶ Following the manufacturer's instructions, apply the fusing web to the wrong side of the base fabric.

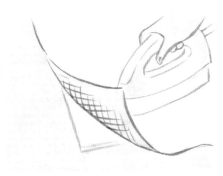

3 ▶ Place one card base piece on the ironing board. Remove the paper backing from the fabric and centre the fabric, right side up, on the card. Fuse it in place, taking care not to iron over the edges.

4 ▶ Turn the card wrong side up. Wrap each corner over the card, and fuse it in place.

5 ▶ Wrap the straight edges of the fabric to the back of the card, and fuse in place.

6 ▶ Glue the wadding to one side of each card side piece.

7 ▶ Lay a fabric side piece wrong side up, and position a card piece, wadding side down, in the centre of the fabric. Wrap one long straight edge of the fabric over the edge of the card, and glue it in place. Repeat on the other side piece.

8 ▶ On the remaining long edge and two short edges of the card, about 2.5cm (1in) in, apply fabric glue. Place the card on one side edge of the base piece with the fabric-

74

covered edge towards the centre and the other edges aligned. Allow the glue to dry. Repeat with the other side pieces.

9 ▸ Turn the base wrong side up. Wrap each corner of the fabric to the back of the card, and glue it in place. Then glue the straight edges in place.

10 ▸ Take the remaining base piece and glue it to the back of the main piece, hiding all cut edges of the fabrics. Place weights, such as heavy books, over the blotter overnight to help the glued layers to bond. Insert the paper blotter.

To cover the file folder:

11 ▸ Following the cutting dimensions, cut one front and one back from thin card. Cut one front fabric piece following the straight grain and a back piece following the bias grain. Cut a back piece from wadding.

12 ▸ Glue the wadding to one side of the back card piece.

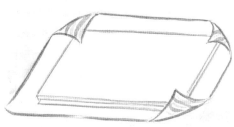

13 ▸ Wrap the card pieces in the fabric and glue the fabric edges to the wrong side, beginning with the corners, then gluing the straight edges.

14 ▸ Glue the centre of the ribbon to the back of the file folder. Glue the front card piece to the front of the file folder and the back piece to the back, over the ribbon. Place the file under weights to dry overnight. Tie the ribbon in a bow, and trim the ends as necessary.

These no-sew desk accessories are easy to make and will brighten up your home office.

NOTICE BOARD

Every home needs a notice board – a place to display favourite photographs, mementoes and reminder notes. This one requires no sewing skills.

C H E C K L I S T

Materials

2 coordinating furnishing fabrics
Satin ribbon
2 pieces thick card
Lightweight wadding
Upholstery tacks
Picture-mounting equipment
Paper-backed fusing web and fabric glue
Scalpel and board for cutting

Techniques

Making patterns and cutting
shapes   pp. 16–17
Fusing fabric   pp. 24–25

Measuring up

Measure the width and length of the board.

Cutting sizes

Base Use the scalpel to cut one piece of card to the desired size.
Top Cut the other piece of card 7.5cm (3in) less than the base in both directions. Trim 4cm (1½in) off all the corners at a 45-degree angle.
Base Fabric Cut the background fabric 15cm (6in) greater than the base in both directions.
Backing Fabric and Fusing Web Cut to the same size as the base.
Top Fabric Cut this 7.5cm (3in) greater than the top in both directions.
Wadding Cut to the same size as the top.

1 ▶ Place the base fabric wrong side up, and position the base card in the centre. Fold one corner of the fabric diagonally over the card, and glue it in place. Repeat this for the remaining corners.

2 ▶ Wrap the straight edges of the fabric to the back of the card, and glue them in place.

3 ▶ Following the manufacturer's instructions, apply the fusing web to the wrong side of the backing fabric. Remove the paper backing, and apply the web-backed fabric to the back of the card.

4 ▶ Glue the wadding to one side of the top card.

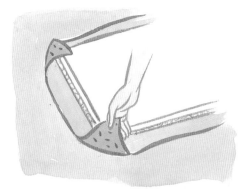

5 ▶ Lay the top fabric wrong side up, and position the top board, wadding side down, in the centre. Wrap one corner of the fabric to the back of the card and glue it in place. Repeat for the remaining corners.

6 ▶ Wrap the straight edges of the fabric to the back of the card, and glue in place.

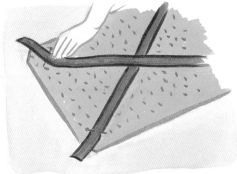

7 Turn the top card right side up. Cut two pieces of ribbon long enough to reach from one corner to the one diagonally opposite, allowing a little extra length. Pin them in place.

8 Cut four more pieces of ribbon, each about two-thirds the length of the first two. Position these ribbons on the card, parallel to the front two, spacing them as shown on the right.

9 Turn the top card over, and glue the ribbon tails to the back of the card.

10 Glue the top card to the centre of the base card with right sides facing up.

11 Apply glue to the stem of each upholstery tack and push into place at the intersection of the ribbons. Glue the picture-mounting equipment to the back of the board.

Make this notice board from a fabric that matches your furniture or curtains to give a coordinated look to your room. If the board is for office use, it could match the desk accessories on page 74.

PADDED PICTURE FRAMES

Economical, colourful frames can easily be made from fabric and pre-cut framing mounts.

C H E C K L I S T

Materials

Furnishing fabric
Picture frame mount
Stiff card
Lightweight wadding
Narrow ribbon
Paper-backed fusing web
Optional lace trimming or piping
Scalpel and cutting board

Techniques

Cutting shapes	pp. 16–17
Fusing fabric	pp. 24–25

Measuring up

Measure the width and length of the pre-cut mount. Measure the inside and outside perimeters of the mount.

Cutting sizes

Base The dimensions are identical to those of the mount without the centre opening.
Easel Stand The width of the stand is 8cm (3in). The length (height of the picture frame) is equal to three-quarters the length of the mount.
Wadding The dimensions are identical to those of the base.
Fabric Covers and Fusing Web Cut the width and length 10cm (4in) greater than the base.
Fabric Easels and Fusing Web Cut the width and length 5cm (2in) greater than the stand.

1 Following the cutting dimensions, cut one base and one easel stand from the stiff card. Cut three fabric covers and two fabric easel pieces. Cut two covers from the fusing web and one mount cover from the wadding. You will also need the purchased mount itself.

2 Place the mount on the wadding. Trace the outline of the centre opening on the wadding, and cut it out. Glue the wadding to one side of the mount.

3 Lay one fabric cover wrong side up, and place the mount in the centre. Trace the centre opening on the fabric.

4 Remove the mount, and draw a line approximately 2.5cm (1in) inside the perimeter of the traced opening. Cut the fabric along the inside line, and cut into each of the corners.

5 Lay the fabric wrong side up again, and place the mount, wadding side down, on top. Fold and glue the inside edges of the fabric to the wrong side of the mount.

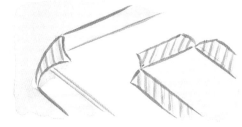

6 Fold each outer corner of fabric diagonally over the mount, and glue it in place.

7 Glue the straight outside edges of the fabric to the wrong side of the mount.

8 Apply optional lace trimming or piping to the wrong side of the mount along the inner and outer edges. Glue the heading to the mount, and allow the decorative edge to extend over the edge.

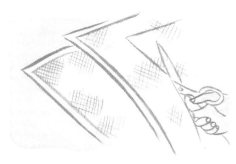

9 Following the manufacturer's instructions, apply the fusing web to the remaining two fabric covers. On one cover, trace the perimeter of the base onto the paper backing. Trim the cover along the traced line.

10 ▶ Place the base on the ironing board. Remove the paper backing from the larger cover. Centre it, right side up, over the base, and fuse it in place. Avoid taking the iron over the edges.

11 ▶ Turn the base wrong side up. Fold each outer corner diagonally over the board, and fuse it in place.

12 ▶ Wrap the straight edges of the fabric to the wrong side of the board, and fuse in place.

13 ▶ Remove the paper backing from the remaining cover. Place the cover, right side up, on the base, and fuse it in place.

These no-sew picture frames would make a perfect present for a friend, especially if you use a fabric that matches or tones in with their existing decor.

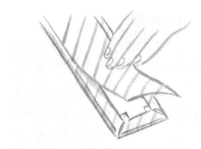

14 ▶ Apply fusing web to the easel stand pieces. Trim one piece, and cover the stand in the same way as described for the base in steps 9–13.

15 ▶ Apply fabric glue to the top 2.5cm (1in) of the easel stand.

Placing lower edges together, and centring the stand, glue the stand to the back of the frame. Allow the glue to dry. Glue a 5cm (2in)-long ribbon between the stand and the frame at the lower edge.

16 ▶ Apply glue to the lower and side edges of the base approximately 1.2cm (½in) from the edges. Glue the front of the frame to the base. Leave the frame under heavy books overnight to let the glue dry thoroughly. Insert photo between the sections from the top of the frame.

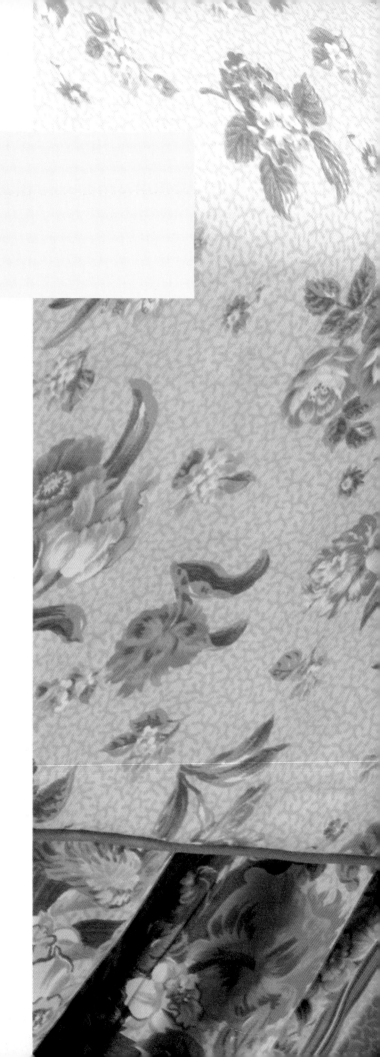

RELAX
IN STYLE

The bed is an ideal place to show
off your favourite fabric. Cover
the bed in one fabric or choose several
coordinating fabrics for valance, quilt
and pillows. Consider the duvet cover
pattern and its companion accessories
for true low-sew soft furnishings. Easy-
to-care for sheets, saturated with colour
are perfect for a child's room. Choose a
bed cover style and a window
treatment from the following projects,
then mix and match fabrics for a
bedroom to be proud of.

GATHERED VALANCE

A pretty striped fabric was chosen for this valance to create the illusion of height.

CHECKLIST

Materials

Furnishing fabric
General sewing equipment

Techniques

Measuring up: beds	pp. 12–13
Joining fabric widths	pp. 14–15
Machine stitching	pp. 22–23

Measuring up

Measure the width and length of the box spring. Measure the two lengths plus the width of the box spring for the three-sided perimeter measurement. Measure the drop from the edge of the box spring to the floor.

Cutting sizes

Deck For the cutting width, add 2.5cm (1in) to the measured width of the box spring. For the cutting length, add 6cm (2½in) to the measured length of the box spring.
Skirt For the cutting length of the skirt, multiply the three-sided perimeter measurement by 6cm (2½in). For the cutting width of the skirt, add 15cm (6in) to the measured drop.
Piece widths of fabric together if necessary to get the right cutting dimensions.
The finished valance will sit 1.2cm (½in) above the floor.
Cutting sizes include 1.2cm (½in) seam allowance.

1 ▸ Following the cutting dimensions, cut one deck and one skirt. Turn up 5cm (2in) on the short upper edge of the deck. Tuck the cut edge in to meet the fold and press again. Topstitch the double hem along the inside fold.

2 ▸ Turn under and press 15cm (6in) on the lower long edge of the skirt. Tuck the cut edge in to meet the fold and press again. Stitch the double hem along the inside fold.

3 ▸ On the short ends of the skirt, turn under and press 5cm (2in). Tuck the cut edge in to meet the fold and press again. Stitch the double hem along the inside fold.

4 ▸ Fold the skirt crosswise into four equal sections. Mark the cut edge at the folds with safety pins.

5 ▸ Using one of the recommended gathering methods, work stitching along the cut edge of the skirt section. Start and stop the stitches at the safety pins, leaving long threads. Pull threads (or cord) gently to gather the skirt section.

6 Divide the three-sided perimeter of the deck by four to get four equal sections. Mark these distances on the deck edge with safety pins.

7 Matching the safety pin markers, pin the skirt to the deck with right sides together and cut edges matching. Distribute the fullness evenly, and pin the skirt to the deck. Stitch and neaten the seams.

One continuous frill skirts three sides of the bed. Hemming this frill could be made easier by using fusing web if you prefer using an iron to using a sewing machine.

PIPED BED SET

Commercial piping gives this quilt and pillowcase their tailored styling.

CHECKLIST

Materials

Furnishing fabric
1.2cm (½in)-diameter purchased piping
Medium-weight wadding
Lightweight wadding for pillowcase
General sewing equipment

Techniques

Measuring up: beds	pp. 12–13
Joining fabric widths	pp. 14–15
Machine and hand stitching	pp. 22–23
Applying trimmings	pp. 16–17
Fusing fabrics	pp. 24–25

Measuring up

Measure the width and length of the mattress. Determine the required drop of the quilt from the top edge of the mattress. A drop is equal to the thickness of the mattress plus 15cm–20cm (6in–8in) – in this case 38cm (15in).
For the pillowcase, measure the width and length of the pillow.

Making the pattern

For the comforter:
Cover and Lining For the cutting width, take the width of the mattress and add twice the drop measurement plus 2.5cm (1in). For the cutting length, take the length of the mattress and add the drop plus 2.5cm (1in).

For the pillowcase:
Front For the cutting width and length add 18cm (7in) to the pillow width and length
Back For the cutting width, add 18cm (7in) to the width of the pillow. For the cutting length, multiply the length of the pillow by 2 and add 24cm (9½in).
Cutting sizes include 1.2cm (½in) seam allowance.

To make the quilt:

1 Following the cutting dimensions, cut one each of the cover, lining and wadding. Piece several widths of fabric together, if necessary, to achieve the cutting dimensions.

2 To create the rounded corners at the lower end of the quilt, use a dinner plate as a template. Position it at the two lower corners, trace around it, and trim the fabric along the lines. Using the quilt top as a pattern, trim the lining and the wadding to match.

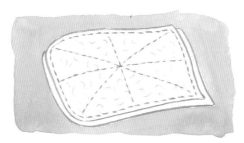

3 Pin the wadding to the wrong side of the top piece. Machine-tack the layers together 1cm (⅜in) from all edges. To prevent shifting, especially on a large quilt, hand-tack the wadding to the quilt top in a star-burst pattern.

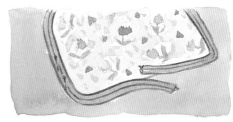

4 With the cut edges even, pin the piping to the right side of the quilt top along all edges. Cut the ends of the piping so that they overlap slightly.

5 Using a needle or sharp-pointed scissors, remove the stitches to approximately 4cm (1½in) from one end of the piping, and fold back the fabric. Trim the covered end and the uncovered end of the cord so that they butt together. Turn under about 1.2cm (½in) on the edge of the overlapping fabric, and wrap the fabric around the join. Pin the ends together.

6 Using the sewing machine zipper foot attachment, stitch the piping to the quilt on all edges.

7 Pin the lining to the quilt top along all edges, placing right sides together. Stitch, leaving an opening of about 50cm (20in) in one side.

8 Turn the quilt right side out. Close the opening using slipstitch. Press flat.

9 Pin 20 to 30 straight or safety pins to the quilt top at random. At each pin, work several small, nearly invisible hand stitches to hold all the layers together. Remove the star-burst tacking stitches.

To make the pillowcase:

10 From the furnishing fabric, cut one front and two back pieces. From the wadding, cut one front. Round off the edges of the pillowcase front following the instructions in step 2. Use the front as a pattern to cut the wadding and the pillowcase backs, giving these two rounded outer corners.

11 Pin the quilt wadding to the wrong side of the pillowcase front. Tack the layers together.

12 Measure and mark 9cm (3½in) from all edges of the right side of the pillowcase front.

13 Attach the piping to the pillowcase following steps 5–7.

14 On the straight inside edge of each back piece, turn under and press 10cm (4in). Tuck the cut edge in to meet the fold and press again. Topstitch the double hem along the inside fold.

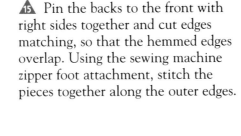

15 Pin the backs to the front with right sides together and cut edges matching, so that the hemmed edges overlap. Using the sewing machine zipper foot attachment, stitch the pieces together along the outer edges.

16 Turn the pillowcase right side out. Press flat. Pin all the layers together along the marked line. Check the back of the pillowcase to make sure the hemmed edges are lying flat. Topstitch through all layers along the marked line.

This quilt uses two coordinating furnishing fabrics to make a surprising reversible feature.

MOCK PLEAT VALANCE

You can make this mock-pleated valance without pressing a single fold.

CHECKLIST

Materials

2 coordinating furnishing fabrics
Fabric for deck and flap lining
General sewing equipment

Techniques

Measuring up: beds	pp. 12–13
Joining fabric widths	pp. 14–15
Machine stitching	pp. 22–23

Measuring up

Measure the width and length of the box spring. Measure the drop of the valance from the box spring to the floor.

Cutting sizes

Decide on the width and number of flaps needed for the sides and the foot of the bed by dividing the box spring width and length by 2, 3 or 4, depending upon the size of the bed. The finished width of the flaps should be 40cm–50cm (16in–20in). The side and foot flaps may be different widths.
Deck For the cutting width, add 2.5cm (1in) to the box spring width. For the cutting length, add 6cm (2½in) to the box spring length.
Side and Foot Flaps For the cutting width, add 2.5cm (1in) to the finished width of the flaps.
Under Panels The cutting width of all under panels is 48cm (19in).
For the cutting length of all flaps and panels, add 2.5cm (1in) to the measured drop. The finished valance will sit 1.2cm (½in) above the floor.
Piece widths of fabric together if necessary to get the right cutting dimensions.
Cutting sizes include 1.2cm (½in) seam allowance.

1 Cut one deck. Cut the number of previously determined side flaps, foot flaps, and under panels, plus a lining for each.

2 Turn under and press 5cm (2in) on the head edge of the deck. Tuck the cut edge in to meet the fold and press again. Topstitch the double hem along the inside fold.

3 Use a large plate as a template to round off the two corners at the lower edge of the deck. Place it on each corner with the edges of the plate even with the fabric edges. Trace the curve of the plate, and trim the fabric along the traced line.

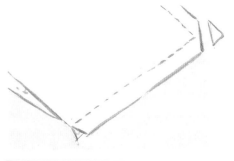

To make a flap or under panel:

4 Pin flap and lining piece together with right sides facing, and stitch around the side and lower edges. Trim the seams and cut across the corners. Press the seams open.

Note: A slightly larger seam allowance may be necessary on the flaps because of the shortened perimeter of the deck caused by rounding off the lower corners.

5 Turn the flap right side out, and press flat. Machine tack the layers together 1cm (⅜in) from the edge. Repeat for all the flaps and under the panels.

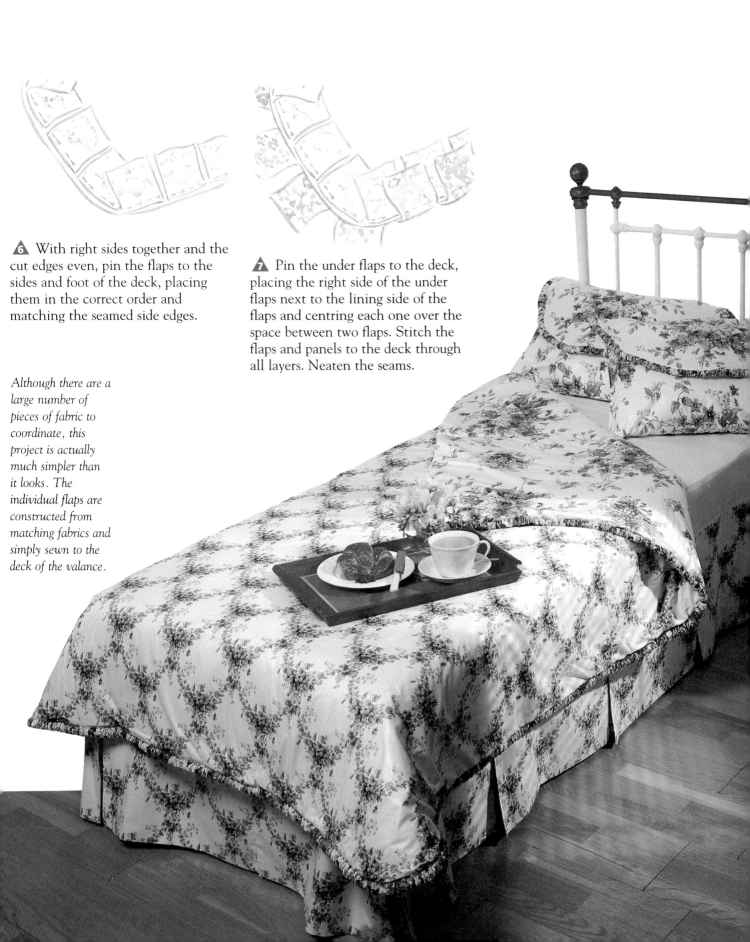

6 With right sides together and the cut edges even, pin the flaps to the sides and foot of the deck, placing them in the correct order and matching the seamed side edges.

7 Pin the under flaps to the deck, placing the right side of the under flaps next to the lining side of the flaps and centring each one over the space between two flaps. Stitch the flaps and panels to the deck through all layers. Neaten the seams.

Although there are a large number of pieces of fabric to coordinate, this project is actually much simpler than it looks. The individual flaps are constructed from matching fabrics and simply sewn to the deck of the valance.

SHIRRED-EDGE QUILT

Custom-made shirred piping adds a contemporary touch to this quilt.

CHECKLIST

Materials

3 coordinating furnishing fabrics
Medium-weight wadding
2.5cm (1in)-wide piping cord
General sewing equipment

Techniques

Measuring up: beds	pp. 12–13
Joining fabric widths	pp. 14–15
Machine stitching	pp. 22–23
Applying trimmings	pp. 16–17
Hand stitching	pp. 22–23

Measuring up

Measure the width and length of the mattress. Determine the required drop of the quilt from the edge of the mattress. A drop is equal to the thickness of the mattress plus 15–20cm (6–8in) – in this case, 38cm (15in).

Cutting sizes

Cover and Lining For the cutting width, add twice the drop measurement to the mattress width plus 5cm (2in). For the cutting length, add the drop measurement to the mattress length.
Bias Strip for Piping The cutting width is 13cm (5in). Add twice the cutting length to the cutting width to get the perimeter around three sides of the quilt. Multiply by 2 to get the cutting length of the strip.
Piping Cord Cut to equal the three-sided perimeter.
Piece several widths of fabric together, if necessary, to achieve the cutting dimensions. Cutting sizes include 2.5cm (1in) seam allowance (the extra width simplifies the piping application).

1 Following the cutting dimensions, cut one main piece each of the cover and lining fabrics. Cut another main piece from wadding. Cut and piece the strips for the piping from the third fabric, following the bias grain.

2 Use a dinner plate as a template to create the rounded corners at the lower end of the cover piece. Position it at each of the two adjacent corners at one long end. Trace round the plate and trim the fabric along the marked lines. Using the cover as a pattern, trim the lining and the wadding to match.

3 Using an erasable pen on the right side of the cover, measure and mark a quilting line 64cm (25in) from the side and lower edges. Mark additional lines, parallel to the first, if you want more quilting or if the quilt is very large.

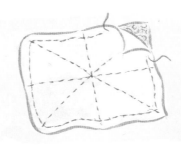

4 Pin the wadding to the wrong side of the cover. Machine-tack the layers together 1cm (⅜in) from all

edges. To prevent shifting, especially on a large quilt, hand-tack the wadding to the quilt cover in a starburst pattern, using long running stitches.

5 Fold the bias strip in half lengthwise at each end. Pin and stitch the ends of the strip together. Trim the seam and turn the ends right side out.

6 Place one end of the piping cord in one end of the strip and secure with a few hand stitches, taking them through the cord and fabric.

7 Wrap the strip around the cord with the cut edges even. Using the zipper foot on the machine and taking 2.5cm (1in) seam allowance, stitch alongside the cord for about 30cm (12in). Stop the machine, leaving the needle in and the presser foot on the fabric.

8 Pull gently on the cord, allowing the fabric behind the presser foot to shirr on it. Stitch for another 30cm (12in), then stop and shirr the fabric onto the cord. Continue until all the fabric fits on the cord, stopping 15cm (6in) from the end. Leave the end unstitched for adjustment later. Pin the uncovered cord to the fabric, taking care not to lose the cord end in the shirring. Except for the last few centimetres (inches), distribute the fullness of the fabric evenly on the cord.

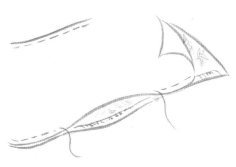

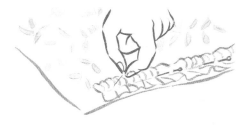

9 Placing the cut edges together, pin the piping to the right side of the quilt along the side and lower edges, beginning and ending 2.5cm (1in) from the top edge. At the end, cut the cord if necessary to fit the quilt. Sew the cord to the fabric strip as in step 6 to secure. Redistribute the fullness.

10 Using the zipper foot on the machine, and again taking 2.5cm (1in) seam allowance, stitch the piping to the quilt.

11 Placing right sides together, pin and stitch the lining to the cover along all edges, again taking 2.5cm (1in) seam allowance and leaving a 75cm (30in) opening in one side edge. Trim the seam and cut across the corners.

12 Turn the quilt right side out through the opening. Close the opening edges with slipstitch. Press the edges flat.

13 Following the marked quilting line, pin and stitch through all the layers. Remove the star-burst tacking stitches.

An extra-wide seam allowance is the secret of applying shirred piping. It reduces twisting and simplifies application.

ADULT BEDROOMS

The possibilities for a bedroom are enormous. It is a place where you can really allow the imagination to run riot. Matching linens, wildly contrasting patterns or plain colours, traditional, modern or opulently fantastic – feel free to furnish the room exactly to your own taste.

The frills and lace are subtly offset in white against the rich cream of the matching linens. Fringes and ribbons give extra texture.

Various types of checks give a traditional atmosphere. Floral patterns and frills soften the straight, geometric lines.

This simple, curved wooden frame produces an exotic, eastern effect. The piles of cushions emphasise this idea.

*The small number
of colours used in
the fabrics unites
the varied
patterning and
prevents it
from being
uncomfortable to
the eye.*

QUICK AND EASY QUILT

The quickest way to make an appealing quilt is by using cushion panel fabric.

C H E C K L I S T

Materials

Cushion pillow fabric
Fabric for binding and backing
Lightweight wadding
Contrasting thread for quilting
General sewing equipment

Techniques

Joining fabric widths	pp. 14–15
Cutting the shapes	pp. 16–17
Machine stitching	pp. 22–23
Hand stitching	pp. 22–23

Measuring up

First measure the width and height of one block of the fabric's design. Also measure the lattice strips between the blocks. On a sheet of paper, make a rough sketch of the quilt, and add up the block and lattice strip measurements to determine the size of the visible face of the cover – the main centre section. Be sure to allow for strips around the outer blocks. Add 4cm (1½in) to all edges. This is the finished size – width and height – of the quilt; record these measurements.

Cutting sizes

Cover Cut two fabric widths, adding 1.2cm (½in) to each for the centre seam. Join them, and press the centre seam open.
Wadding Cut wadding the same size as cover.
Backing Add 11.5cm (4½in) to the visible face measurements of the cover. Piece widths, as necessary, to achieve the required size.

1 ▷ Trim the edges of the cover and backing, if necessary, to make them the correct sizes.

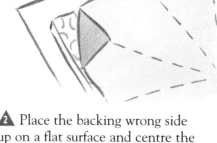

2 Place the backing wrong side up on a flat surface and centre the wadding on top. Lay the cover on top of the wadding, with the edges even. Pin and hand-tack the layers together in a star-burst pattern.

3 Select the parts of the printed design that you would like to feature, and hand-quilt all the layers together along the chosen lines. Use a small, even running stitch and ordinary sewing or quilting thread. The lines of stitching should be no less than 2.5cm (1in) and no more than 30cm (12in) apart.

4 On all edges, and beginning in the middle of one side, turn up the backing 4cm (1½in) so that the cut edge meets the wadding edge. Turn up 4cm (1½in) again, and pin the folded edge of the backing to the quilt cover. Press the edges lightly.

5 At each corner, open out the binding edges and trim off the corner about 5cm (2in) from the point. Turn up the first fold, as in step 4, then fold in the binding corner diagonally, so that the fold touches the corner of the wadding and cover fabric.

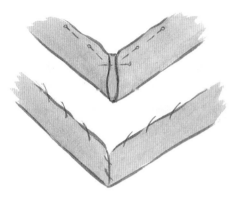

6 ▶ Turn up the second fold in the binding so that the diagonal edges meet at the corner, forming a mitred fold. Pin the binding in place.

7 ▶ Slipstitch the edges of the binding to the cover, and slipstitch the diagonal corners together.

FINDING THE RIGHT FABRIC

If cushion panel fabric is unavailable, similar results can be achieved with dressmaker or furnishing fabric, or even a sheet, so long as it has a large repeating pattern. Draw a square or rectangle around a selected motif, and add 1.2cm (½in) to all edges. If the seam allowances encroach on the next motif, use every alternate motif. Sew the identical-sized blocks together in strips, then join the strips, and proceed with the quilt as instructed.

The most effective quilts are those with strong tonal contrasts and a striking repeated motif which creates the illusion of real patchwork or appliqué.

PINKED-EDGE CUSHIONS

The crisp edges of these cushions are achieved with fusing web and a pair of pinking shears.

CHECKLIST

Materials

2 coordinated furnishing fabrics
Square cushion pad
Paper-backed fusing web
General sewing equipment

Techniques

Machine stitching	pp. 22–23
Fusing fabric	pp. 24–25

Measuring up

Measure the width/length of the cushion pad.

Cutting size

For the cutting size, add 20cm (8in) to the cushion pad size in both directions.

1▶ Following the cutting dimensions, cut one square from each of the two fabrics. Cut four rectangles of fusing web, each 10cm (4in) wide by the cutting width/length of the cover.

2▶ Using an air-soluble or water-soluble pen, measure and mark a 10cm (4in) border along all edges on the right side of the top cover.

3▶ Following the manufacturer's instructions, apply fusing web to the wrong side of the top along all edges, trimming the ends of the web so that they fit around the square without overlapping. Remove the paper backing.

4▶ On the right side of the top, insert a pin at one marked line.

5▶ Place the top and bottom cover pieces on the ironing board with wrong sides together and edges matching. Fuse together the three unmarked edges. Do not fuse the fourth, pinned, edge of the cover.

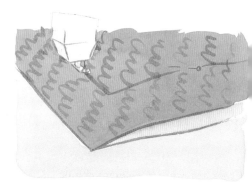

6▶ Stitch the top to the bottom, following the marked lines on the fused edges of the cover and backstitching at the ends to secure. Do not stitch along the pinned line.

7▶ Remove the marker pin, and insert the cushion pad in the cover through the opening.

8 ► With the cut edges even, pin the top and bottom of the cover together along the open, marked line.

9 ► Using the sewing machine zipper foot attachment, stitch along the marked line; backstitch at the ends to secure.

10 ► Holding the cushion up at an angle to the ironing board, fuse together the remaining part of the border.

11 ► Trim 1.2cm (½in) from all the edges using pinking shears.

Quick and easy cushions like these will brighten up even the dullest corner. Try adding some iron-on appliqués, ribbon, or lace for a different decorative effect.

TASSEL-PELMET CURTAIN

The diagonal lines of the pelmet give these curtains a style and elegance that would grace any bedroom or sitting room.

C H E C K L I S T

Materials

Furnishing fabric
Large tassels
General sewing equipment

Techniques

Machine stitching   pp. 22–23

Measuring up

Measure the window frame between its outside edges. Measure the length from the pole to the sill and the pole to the floor. The finished length of the pelmet is one-third of the distance from the top of the pole to the sill, and the finished length of the curtain is the distance from the top of the pole to the floor.

Cutting sizes

Curtain Panel For the cutting length, add 10cm (4in) to the finished length.
Pelmet For the cutting length, add 6cm (2½in) to the finished length. For the cutting width of each curtain panel and pelmet, add 10cm (4in) to the measured window width. Piece several widths together, if necessary, to get the right cutting widths.
The curtains will have a 2 : 1 fullness ratio and will sit 1.2cm (½in) above the floor. Cutting sizes include 1.2cm (½in) seam allowance.

To make one panel:

1 At the lower edge of the pelmet, mark the centre point. Draw a line from the mark to each corner at the upper edge of the pelmet. Cut along the line.

2 Turn under and press 5cm (2in) on one side edge of the pelmet. Tuck the cut edge in to meet the fold, and press again. Topstitch the double hem along the inside fold. Repeat for the other side edge.

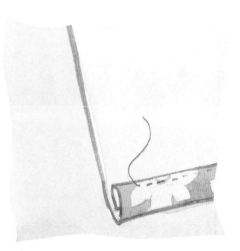

3 Turn under and press 10cm (4in) on the lower edge of the curtain. Tuck the cut edge in to meet the fold, and press again. Stitch the double hem along the inside fold.

4 Turn under and press 5cm (2in) on each side edge of the curtain. Tuck the cut edge in to meet the fold, and press again. Topstitch the double hem along the inside fold.

5 Pin the pelmet to the curtain along the upper edges, with the right side of the pelmet facing the wrong side of the curtain and the cut edges matching; stitch. Press open and neaten the seam.

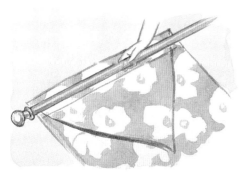

6 Turn the pelmet over to the right side of the curtain. Press the seam flat. On the right side of the pelmet, measure and mark 8cm (3in), or a dimension equal to the diameter of your curtain pole, plus a little extra for ease, from the seam.

7 Pin and stitch through all the layers along the marked line, backstitching at the ends to secure.

8 Sew a tassel to the point of the pelmet.

A pelmet adds an attractive finishing touch to what otherwise would be ordinary curtains. It is simple to make and the addition of a readymade tassel makes it extra special.

To make this an even simpler two-seam project, use fusing web for all of the hemming in steps 2–4.

TAB AND SWAG CURTAINS

Gauze fabric gives a light and airy feeling to these curtains. The extra-long tabs help to show off a decorative pole.

CHECKLIST

Materials

Coordinating gauze or other sheer fabrics
General sewing equipment

Techniques

Joining fabric widths	pp. 14–15
Machine stitching	pp. 22–23
Measuring up: windows	pp. 12–13
Installing window treatments	pp. 24–25

Measuring up

Measure the width of the window frame, between its outside edges, and the length from pole to floor. Use cord to determine the swag length. Drape the cord over the pole at one end, create a swag, and pass it over the pole at the other end. Measure the cord.

Cutting sizes

Curtain Panel For the cutting width, add 10cm (4in) to the window width. For the cutting length, subtract 6cm (2½in) from the window length.
Tabs Cut each tab 10cm x 56cm (4in x 22in).
Swag Panel The cutting width equals the fabric width. For the cutting length, add 10cm (4in) to the cord measurement.
Piece several widths of fabric together, if necessary, to achieve the total panel width. When closed, the curtain will have 2:1 fullness and will hang 1.2cm (½in) above the floor.
Cutting sizes include 1.2cm (½in) seam allowance.

1▶ Following the cutting dimensions, cut two swag panels, two curtain panels and enough tabs to allow 18–25cm (7–10in) spacing between each at the top of the panels.

2▶ To make the curtain panels: turn under and press 10cm (4in) on the upper and lower edges of each panel. Tuck the cut edge in to meet the fold and press again. Topstitch the double hem along the inside fold.

3▶ On the side edge of each panel turn under and press to wrong side. Tuck the cut edge in to meet the fold and press again. Topstitch the double hem along the inside fold.

To make the tabs:

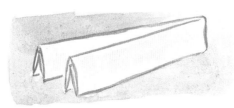

4▶ Fold the tab in half lengthwise with wrong sides facing, and press. Open up and fold the cut edges so that they meet in the centre along the line of the first fold. Now fold this in half again, enclosing the cut edges, and press. Fold the tab in half so that the short edges meet, and stitch close to the folded edges through all eight layers. Repeat for the other tabs.

5▶ Turn under and press 1.2cm (½in) on both ends of the tab. Fold the tab in half crosswise, enclosing the cut ends, and pin the ends together. Repeat for each of the remaining tabs.

6▶ Spacing evenly, measure and mark the tab positions on the wrong side of the curtain, 1.2cm (½in) from the top edge.

7▶ Matching the hemmed ends to the marked tab positions, pin and stitch the tabs to the wrong side of the curtain at the upper edge.

To make the swag panels:

▶ **8** On the two long edges of the swag panel, turn under and press 5cm (2in). Tuck the cut edge in to meet the fold and press again. Stitch along the second fold.

▶ **9** On the two short ends of the panel, turn under and press 5cm (2in). Tuck the cut edge in to meet the fold and press again. Stitch close to the second fold.

10 In a large room or a long hallway, fold the panel lengthwise in soft, concertina-style pleats approximately 23cm (9in) wide. The two long hemmed edges should begin and end at the same side of the folded stack. Do not press the pleats.

11 ▶ For very long swags, pin the stack together with extra-large safety pins. Carry the fabric to the window and drape it over the pole in the same fashion as the cord, with the long hemmed edges facing the wall.

This graceful window dressing, which works without the use of curtain hooks, will add elegance to any room. The sewing could be reduced by using fusing web to hem the curtain and swag panels.

CUSHION-TOPPED OTTOMAN

Make this loose cover to improve upon an existing ottoman or cover a wooden stool for added comfort.

C H E C K L I S T

Materials

Furnishing fabric
Medium-weight wadding
General sewing equipment

Techniques

Joining fabric widths	pp. 14–15
Machine stitching	pp. 22–23

Measuring up

Measure the width and length of the ottoman and the height from the top edge to the floor.

Cutting sizes

Top For the cutting width and length, add 2.5cm (1in) to the width and length of the ottoman.
Side skirt pieces For the cutting length, add 43cm (17in) to the measured length.
End skirt pieces For the cutting length, add 43cm (17in) to the measured width. For the cutting width of all skirts, add 5cm (2in) to the height of the ottoman.
NOTE: If the ottoman is square, all four skirt pieces will be the same width.
Cushion For the cutting width and length, add 8cm (3in) to the width and length of the ottoman.
Cushion Ties Cut each cushion tie 8cm x 30cm (3in x 12in).
The finished skirt will sit 1.2cm (½in) above floor.
Cutting sizes include 1.2cm (½in) seam allowance.

1 Following the cutting dimensions, cut one top; two each of skirt sides, skirt ends, and cushion cover; and eight cushion ties.

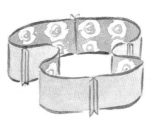

2 With right sides facing, stitch the sides and ends of the skirt together, alternating sides and ends to create one continuous loop of fabric. Press all of the seams open and neaten the edges.

3 Neaten the one long edge of the skirt. Turn under and press 5cm (2in) on this edge. Sew the hem in place by hand or machine.

4 Locate each of the seams joining the skirt sections. On the right side of the fabric, measure and mark parallel lines 10cm (4in) and 20cm (8in) to each side of each seam.

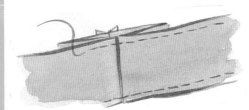

5 Matching the marks, press an inverted pleat at each seam. Machine or hand-tack the pleat 5mm (¼in) from the cut edge.

6 Turn under and press 1.2cm (½in) on one short end of one tie. Turn under and press 1.2cm (½in) on the two side edges.

7 Fold the tie in half lengthwise with wrong sides and folded edges together. Topstitch close to the fold along the long and short edges. Repeat steps 6 and 7 for all ties.

8 Mark the mid-point of each edge of the ottoman top. With the cut edges even, pin and stitch a tie to each mark on the right side of the fabric.

9 Pin the skirt to the ottoman top, placing right sides together and matching the pleats with the corners.

To simplify turning the corners, cut diagonally across the corners, and clip the pleat at the seamline up to the tacking stitches. Stitch the seam, taking care not to catch the loose ends of the ties in the seam. Neaten the seam edges.

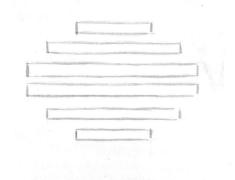

To make the cushion:

10▶ Mark the mid-point of each edge on one cushion piece. Pin and stitch a tie to each mark on the right side of the cushion, placing cut edges together.

11▶ Place the two cushion pieces together with right sides facing. Pin and stitch around the edges, leaving almost all of one edge open. Avoid catching the loose ends of the ties in the seam.

12▶ Turn cushion right side out. Cut two pieces of wadding the same size as the cushion and two more pairs, grading each pair to be 5cm (2in) smaller than the previous size. Place all six layers together, with the smallest pieces at the top and bottom and larger pieces in the centre. Loosely tack the wadding layers together.

13▶ Insert the wadding into the cushion cover, and close the opening with slipstitch.

14▶ Attach the cushion to the top of the ottoman cover by tying each pair of ties in a reef knot.

Inverted pleats at the four corners give a crisply tailored look to this ottoman loose cover.

DUVET COVER

Only two bed sheets, three seams and a few buttonholes are needed to complete a cosy duvet cover.

CHECKLIST

Materials

2 bed sheets
5 large buttons
Purchased duvet
General sewing equipment

Techniques

Measuring up: beds	pp. 12–13
Machine stitching	pp. 22–23

Measuring up

Measure the width and length of the duvet. Measure the width of the mattress; add twice the depth of the mattress plus 36cm (14in). Measure the length of the mattress plus the drop at the foot of the bed; add the depth of the mattress plus 18cm (7in).

Cutting sizes

Top (A) For the cutting width, add 2.5cm (1in) to the measured width of the mattress. For the cutting length, subtract 12cm (4½in) from the measured length.
Bottom (B) For the cutting width, add 2.5cm (1in) to the measured width.
For the cutting length, add 27cm (10½in) to the measured length.
Purchase sheets wide enough to accommodate the cutting width of the cover. Cutting sizes include 1.2cm (½in) seam

1 ▶ Measuring from the hemmed edge of each sheet, mark the cutting length for the top and bottom pieces. Measure and mark the cutting width for each cover piece. Cut along marked lines.

2 ▲ On the bottom, fold 25cm (10in) to the right side along the hemmed edge. Do not press the fold. Machine-tack the side edges together.

3 ▲ Pin the top cover to the bottom cover with right sides facing and cut edges even, so that the top overlaps the turned-over-edge of the bottom piece. Stitch the three cut edges together. Neaten the seams.

4 ▲ Turn the cover right side out. The sheet hem from the bottom cover now appears on the front in an envelope-style flap. Along the centre of the hem, measure 30cm (12in) from each side edge and mark a buttonhole position. Mark three more buttonholes between these two, spacing them evenly and centring them in the hem. Stitch buttonholes in the hem of the cover.

5 ▲ Using pins, mark the button position below each buttonhole on the hidden sheet hem of the cover top. Sew buttons to the hem of the cover top.

FLANGED PILLOWCASE

A pillow is neatly dressed in a ribbon-trimmed pillowcase with a simple envelope-style back opening.

CHECKLIST

Materials

Bed sheet
Fusible interfacing
2cm (¾in)-wide grosgrain ribbon
General sewing equipment

Techniques

Machine stitching	pp. 22–23
Applying trimmings	pp. 16–17

Measuring up

Measure the width and length of the pillow.

Cutting sizes

Front (A) For the cutting width and length, add 18cm (7in) to the measured width and length of the pillow.
Back (B) For the cutting width, add 18cm (7in) to the width of the pillow. For the cutting length, take half the measured length and add 24cm (9½in).
Depending upon the pillow size, the cutting width may now exceed the length.
Cutting sizes include 1.2cm (½in) seam allowance.

1 Cut one front and two back pieces from the sheet and one front piece from the interfacing.

2 Measure and mark 9cm (3½in) from all edges of the pillowcase front on the right side of the fabric. Fuse the ribbon to the front along the inside edge of the marked line, folding in mitred corners and turning under the cut ends to neaten.

3 Fuse the interfacing to the wrong side of the pillowcase front.

4 Lay the two back pieces on the interfaced side of the front piece so that cut edges match and the two inner edges of the back piece overlap. Lift up each piece separately and, on one inner edge, turn under and press

10cm (4in). Tuck the cut edge in to meet the fold and press again. Topstitch the double hem along the inside fold.

5 Reassemble the pieces as in step 4 and pin them together. Stitch the pieces together along all edges. Cut them across the corners and press the seams open.

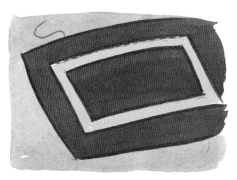

6 Turn the pillowcase right side out through the hemmed opening, and press flat. Pin all the layers together along the applied ribbon. Check the back of the pillowcase to make sure that the flaps are lying flat. Topstitch through all layers along the outer edge of ribbon.

PLEATED VALANCE

Inverted pleats are featured at the sides and lower corners of this low-sew valance.

CHECKLIST

Materials

Bed sheets
2.5cm (1in)-wide grosgrain ribbon
General sewing equipment

Techniques

Measuring up: beds	pp. 12–13
Joining fabric widths	pp. 14–15
Machine stitching	pp. 22–23
Applying trimmings	pp. 16–17

Measuring up

Measure the width and length of the mattress. Measure the drop from the bottom edge of the mattress to the floor.

Cutting sizes

Deck For the cutting width, add 2.5cm (1in) to the mattress width. For the cutting length, add 6.5cm (2½in) to the length.
Upper Skirt For the cutting length of the skirt at the upper sides of the bed, take half the length of the mattress and add 27cm (10½in).
Lower Skirt For the cutting length of the skirt at the lower sides of the bed, take half the length and add 43cm (17in).
Foot Skirt For the cutting length of the skirt at the foot of the bed, add 43cm (17in) to the width.
All skirts For the cutting width, add 10cm (4in) to the measured drop. Piece several widths of fabric together if necessary to get the correct cutting dimensions. The finished skirt will sit 1.2cm (½in) above the floor. Cutting sizes include 1.2cm (½in) seam allowance.

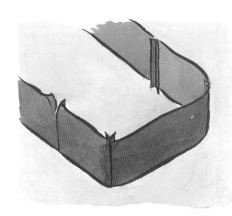

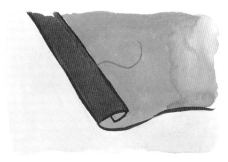

1 Cut one deck, one foot skirt, and two each of the upper and lower skirts. Stitch the upper side, lower side, and foot sections of the skirt together in the correct order, matching the short edges and placing right sides together. Press the seams open and neaten the edges.

2 On each short end of the skirt, turn under and press 5cm (2in). Tuck the cut edge in to meet the fold and press again. Topstitch the double hem along the inside fold.

3 On the lower, long edge of the skirt, turn under and press 10cm (4in). Tuck the cut edge in to meet the fold and press again. Topstitch the double hem along the upper fold. Stitch or fuse the ribbon along the hem, following the stitching line, and turn under 1.2cm (½in) at each end to neaten it.

4 Locate each of the seams joining the upper, lower and foot skirt sections. On the right side of the fabric, measure and mark two parallel lines 10cm (4in) and 20cm (8in) to each side of every seam.

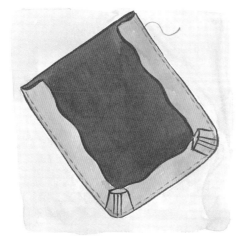

8 Pin the skirt to the side and foot edges of the deck, placing right sides and cut edges together and positioning the pleats at the lower corners and midway along the sides. Stitch and neaten the seams.

5 Fold the fabric along the outer marked lines, wrong sides together; press. Then bring the folds together at the seam and press again, including the inner folds, to make an inverted pleat. Tack the pleat in place 5mm (¼in) from the cut edge.

If bed sheets are used as the fabric, the task of piecing together many fabric widths is eliminated.

7 To round off the two corners at the lower edge of the deck, place a large dinner plate on the corner, aligning it with the fabric edges. Trace the curve of the plate, and trim the fabric along the traced line.

6 Turn under and press 5cm (2in) on the head edge of the deck. Tuck the cut edge in to meet the fold and press again. Topstitch the double hem along the inside fold.

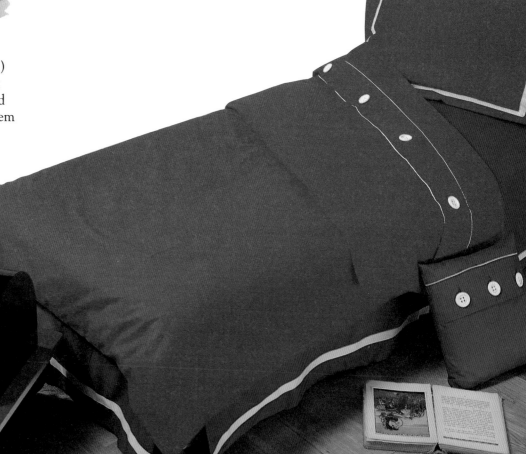

ROPE-TRIMMED CURTAIN

On this curtain, cotton cord looped over a pole is an important element of the design.

CHECKLIST

Materials

Furnishing fabric
Twisted cord
Metal eyelets
Fusible interfacing
General sewing equipment

Techniques

Joining fabric widths	pp. 14–15
Machine stitching	pp. 22–23
Fusing fabric	pp. 24–25

Measuring up

Measure the width and length of the window frame between outside edges and sill. For a shower curtain, measure the width and length of the area to be covered above the bathtub. Standard shower curtains are usually 180cm (70in) square.

Cutting sizes

Curtain Panel For the cutting width, add 30cm (12in) to the measured width of window. For the cutting length, add 12cm (4½in) to the measured length.
Heading The cutting width is 23cm (9in). For the length, add 5cm (2in) to the measured width.
Piece several widths of fabric together if necessary to achieve the total curtain width. When closed, the curtain will hang flat. Cutting sizes include 1.2cm (½in) seam allowance.

1 Following the cutting dimensions, cut one curtain panel and one heading. Also cut one heading from interfacing.

2 Turn under and press 20cm (8in) on the lower edge of the curtain. Tuck cut edge in to meet the fold. Press. Topstitch double hem along inside fold.

3 Turn under and press 15cm (6in) on the side edges of the curtain. Tuck the cut edge in to meet the fold and press again. Topstitch the double hem along the inside fold.

4 Following the manufacturer's instructions, fuse the interfacing to the wrong side of the heading. Turn under and press 1.2cm (½in) on one long edge of the heading.

5 Pin the heading to the curtain right sides together, matching the long cut edges. The heading extends 1.2cm (½in) beyond the hemmed sides of the curtain. Stitch. Press seam allowances towards the heading.

6 Turn the fabric right side up. Bring the edge of the heading down to the stitching line, thus folding the heading in half. Pin the ends together. Using a ruler and the curtain edges as guides, mark the stitching line. Stitch seams; cut across the corners diagonally.

7 Turn the heading right side out. On the wrong side of the curtain, pin the fold of the heading along the stitching line. Topstitch through all layers along the fold.

8▶ Mark the eyelets' positions on the right side of the heading, spacing them 10cm–15cm (4in–6in) apart. The first and last eyelet should be placed either 4cm (1½in) from the side edge or in the centre of the side hem. Fix the eyelets to the curtain.

9▶ Tie a knot 5cm (2in) from one end of the cord, to prevent it from fraying, and tie another 46cm (18in) from it. To determine the distance between knots, lay the curtain flat and position the pole the required distance above it. Using a tape measure, measure the distance from one eyelet to the next, over the pole. Check the amount of cord taken up by a knot and add this to the spacing measurement. Mark this total measurement along the cord the required number of times for the

eyelets (subtracting the knot measurement for the mark following the already tied knot).

10▶ Thread the cord through the first eyelet, from front to back, then through the second. Tie a knot just

after the first mark. Continue in this way until you have a knot at each eyelet.

11▶ After the last eyelet, tie a knot 46cm (18in) along the cord. Cut the cord 5cm (2in) beyond this knot. Fluff out the cord ends on the first and last knots.

Select a striped fabric and use it creatively at the heading of the curtain. Experiment with eyelet and cord sizes to find the right fit. This design is ideal for use in a child's bedroom. It could also make a perfect shower curtain if teamed with a plastic liner.

QUILTED BED COVER

Bright pastels make this channel-stitched quilt an eye-catcher.

C H E C K L I S T

Materials

Furnishing fabric
Lining fabric
Lightweight wadding
2.5cm (1in)-wide double-fold bias tape
General sewing equipment

Techniques

Measuring up: beds	pp. 12–13
Joining fabric widths	pp. 14–15
Machine stitching	pp. 22–23
Applying trimmings	pp. 16–17
Hand stitching	pp. 22–23

Measuring up

Measure the width and length of the mattress. Determine the desired drop of the quilt from the edge of the mattress. A drop is equal to the thickness of the mattress plus 15cm–20cm (6in–8in). For this quilt it measures 38cm (15in).

Cutting sizes

Cover and Lining For the cutting width, multiply the drop measurement by 2; add the mattress width plus 2.5cm (1in). For the cutting length, add the drop measurement to the mattress length plus 2.5cm (1in). Piece several widths of fabric together, if necessary, to achieve the cutting dimensions. Cutting sizes include 1.2cm (½in) seam allowance.

▷ 1 Following the cutting dimensions, cut one piece each of the cover, lining and wadding.

▷ 2 To determine how many quilting lines you will need, divide the cutting width of the quilt by 8. On the right side of the cover and using a ruler and water-soluble pen, measure and mark quilting lines lengthwise on the cover, parallel with the side edges.

▷ 3 Use a dinner plate as a template for the rounded corners at the lower end of the quilt. Position it at each of the two adjacent corners at one long end of the quilt cover, and trace around it. Trim the fabric along the lines. Using the quilt cover as a pattern, trim the lining and wadding pieces at the lower corners only.

▷ 4 Pin the wadding to the wrong side of the cover. Machine-tack all the layers together 1cm (⅜in) from all the edges.

▷ 5 With right sides facing, pin and hand or machine stitch the cover to the lining at the short upper edge.

▷ 6 Trim the wadding from the seam allowance on the stitched edge, and press the seam open. Turn the quilt right side out, so that the wadding lies between the fabric layers.

▷ 7 On the upper edge, pin and topstitch the layers together 2.5cm (1in) from the seamline. Pin the layers together on the side and lower edges.

▷ 8 Hand- or pin-tack all the layers of the quilt together along the lines you have marked.

9▶ Machine stitch through all layers along the marked lines, beginning each time at the seamed upper edge and ending at the lower edge.

10▶ To piece the bias tape along the straight grain, start by opening out the folds. Place two ends together with right sides facing to form a right angle. Mark a straight line at a 45-degree angle across the corner. Stitch the bias strips together along the line. Trim 5mm (¼in) from the stitching line, cutting off the corner.

11▶ Press the seam open, and re-press the manufacturer's folds. Piece together enough bias tape to equal the length of both sides plus the lower edge of the quilt.

Commercial bias tape is a quicker alternative to hand-cut bias tape. Make sure that the tape is in a coordinating colour.

12▶ On one end of the tape, turn under and press 1.2cm (½in). Pin the tape around the side and lower edges of the quilt top, placing right sides together and aligning the outer crease of the tape with the seamline.

13▶ Stitch the tape to the quilt through all layers along the crease of the tape.

14▶ Turn and pin the tape to the wrong side of the quilt, enclosing the cut edge of the quilt. Slipstitch the tape to the lining along the edges (see Basic Stitching Techniques, pp. 22–23).

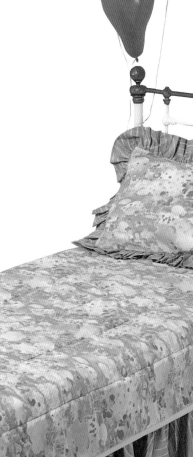

FRILLED PILLOWCASE

Frills frame a pillowcase designed to coordinate with the quilt and valance.

CHECKLIST

Materials

2 coordinating furnishing fabrics
General sewing equipment

Techniques

Joining fabric widths	pp. 14–15
Machine stitching	pp. 22–23

Measuring up

Measure the width and length of the pillow. Add these measurements together and multiply by 2 to get the perimeter.

Cutting sizes

Front (A) For the cutting width and length, add 2.5cm (1in) to the width and length of the pillow.

Back (B) For the cutting width, add 2.5cm (1in) to the width of the pillow. For the cutting length, divide the pillow length by 2 and add 17cm (6½in).

Note: Depending upon the pillow size, the cutting width of the back pieces may exceed the length.

Frill (C) The cutting width is 23cm (9in). For the cutting length, multiply the perimeter by 2½.

Cutting sizes include 1.2cm (½in) seam allowance.

1▶ From the main furnishing fabric, cut one front and two back pieces. From the other fabric, cut one frill following the bias of the fabric. You will probably need to piece several strips together to get the right cutting length.

2▶ Stitch the short ends of the frill together with right sides facing to form a continuous loop. Press the seams open.

3▶ Fold the frill in half lengthwise with wrong sides facing; press the fold. Pin the long cut edges together.

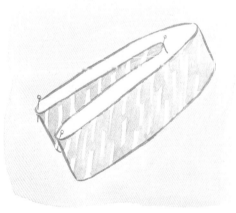

4▶ Fold the frill in half crosswise, then in half again to divide it into four equal sections. Mark the sections along the cut edge.

5▶ Stitch gathering threads along the cut edges of each of the four sections separately (see Basic Stitching Techniques pp. 22–23). Pull the threads gently to gather the frill to approximately half its original length.

6▶ By folding crosswise and lengthwise, divide the pillow front into four equal sections. Mark at the cut edges.

7▶ Matching the markings and placing cut edges together, pin the frill to the right side of the pillow front.

The perfect complement to this bed set, intended for a young girl, is a frilled valance. The insructions are almost the same as those for the gathered valance on page 82. The only difference is that the sides and lower edge of this valance were hemmed and gathered separately before being sewn to the deck.

8 Pull the gathering threads, if necessary, to make the frill fit the pillow front. Distributing the fullness evenly, pin all the edges of the frill in place. Machine tack the frill to the front 1cm (⅜in) from the edges.

9▶ Turn under and press 10cm (4in) on one 'width' edge of each back piece. Tuck the cut edge in to meet the fold and press again. Topstitch the double hem along the inside fold.

10 Pin the backs to the frilled front, placing right sides and cut edges together and overlapping the hemmed edges of the back pieces at the centre. Stitch the pieces together along all outer edges. Trim the seam and cut across the corners.

11▶ Turn the pillowcase right side out through the hemmed opening. Insert the pillow.

For a pillowcase with a little extra body, add a layer of thin wadding under the front section. This project can be simplified further by using fusing web to do the hemming.

BUTTERFLY PELMET

In a matter of minutes, transform two lace-trimmed bed sheets into a pretty butterfly pelmet.

C H E C K L I S T

Materials

2 single bed sheets with decorative hems
3.4m (3¾yd) of 4cm (1½in)-wide ribbon
3.4m (3¾yd) of adhesive 2-cord shirring tape
Fusing web strip 1cm (⅜in) wide
Hook and loop tape
General sewing equipment
Fabric glue
Pelmet board and hardware

Techniques

Measuring up: windows   pp. 12–13
Installing window treatments   pp. 12–13

Measuring up

Measure the width of the window frame between its outside edges. Measure the height of the window.

Cutting sizes

Swag and right tail Divide the window width by 8, subtract one-eighth for the left tail. To the remainder, add one-third of the window height, which is the tail length. The total is the cutting length of the swag and right tail.
Left tail Add the tail length (one-third window length) to one-eighth of the window width. This is the cutting length. The piecing seam joining these two pieces will be concealed by the shirring and ribbon. For a very wide window it may be necessary to use three sheets and also to piece the right-hand side of the pelmet. A seam allowance of 1.2cm (½in) is included.

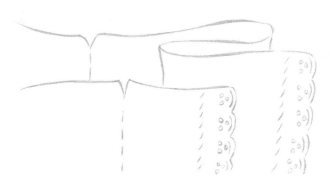

1 Measuring from the decorative hemmed edge of each sheet, mark the cutting length for the swag and right tail on one sheet and the cutting length for the left tail on the other. Cut across each sheet on these lines.

2 Turn under and press the seam allowance on the tail piece. Cut a length of fusing web to fit. Placing the folded tail edge over the swag edge, right sides upwards, and positioning the web in between, fuse them together.

3 The next step is optional, depending on how well the sheet is hemmed. Turn under and press 2.5cm (1in) on each long edge. Tuck the cut edge in to meet the fold. Fuse each hem along the inside fold.

4 Fold the pelmet in half down the middle of the swag with right sides together. Lay it on a flat surface, seamed side down. Pin the two layers together along the seam and, using an erasable pen, trace the seamline onto the swag and tail piece. This marks the position for the shirring tape.

*This luxurious
pelmet looks far
more complex than
it really is; in fact it
is totally 'no sew'.
Fusing web and
adhesive shirring
tape remove the
need to set up the
sewing machine or
thread a needle.*

5 Cut two lengths of shirring tape long enough to reach from the top to the bottom of the pelmet. Centre the tape on the seam and the marked line on the wrong side and fuse it in place. To gather the pelmet, pull up the cords and tie them together.

6 Cut a length of hook and loop tape equal to the window width. Glue the loop (fuzzy) half to the top edge of the pelmet on the wrong side, centring it between the two ends.

7 Staple or glue the hook (stiff) half of the tape to the long back edge on top of the pelmet board.

8 Position the pelmet on the pelmet board and join the hook and loop tapes. Cut the ribbon in two. Slip each piece of ribbon between the hook and loop tape at the top of the shirring and tie it in a bow. Trim the ends as required.

SIMPLE SHOWER CURTAIN

Extra-wide fabric printed with large blocks is a perfect choice for a decorative shower curtain.

CHECKLIST

Materials

Furnishing fabric
Paper-backed 1cm (⅜in)-wide fusing web strip
General sewing equipment

Techniques

Joining fabric widths	pp. 14–15
Machine stitching	pp. 22–23
Fusing fabric	pp. 24–25

Measuring up

Measure the width and length of the space from the curtain rod to halfway down the sides of the bath. Standard shower curtains usually measure 180cm (70in) square.

Cutting sizes

Curtain For the cutting width, add 10cm (4in) to the width of the space. For the cutting length, add 10cm (4in) to the length.
Tabs Cut each tab 10cm x 23cm (4in x 9 in). Piece several widths of fabric together if necessary to set the necessary curtain width. When closed, the curtain will hang flat with no fullness.
Cutting sizes include 1.2cm (½in) seam allowance.

1 Following the cutting dimensions, cut one curtain and enough tabs to allow a 18cm–25cm (7in–10in) spacing between each at the top of the curtain.

2 Turn under and press 5cm (2in) on the upper and lower edges of the curtain. Tuck the cut edge in to meet the fold and press again. Topstitch the double hem along the inside fold. Repeat for the side edges.

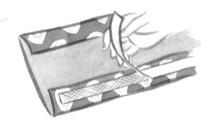

3 Turn under and press 1.2cm (½in) on both long edges of each tab. Following the manufacturer's instructions, apply fusing web to the seam allowance of one edge. Remove the paper backing.

4 Bring over the other edge – with the seam allowance still folded in – to meet the edge with the web. Fuse the two edges together, and press flat.

5 Fold the tab in half crosswise, and pin the ends together.

6 Spacing evenly, measure and mark each tab position on the wrong side of the curtain 2.5cm (1in) from the top edge.

7 Matching the cut ends to the tab positions, pin and sew the tabs to the wrong side of the curtain at the upper edge.

SENSATIONAL SHOWER CURTAINS

Here are some easy and attractive
alternatives to the standard tab shower
curtain.
—Replace fabric tabs with extra-wide
grosgrain ribbon.
—Apply wide broderie anglaise trim to
the tabs.
—Cut each ribbon tab 92cm (36in)
long. Fold in half and sew the folded end
to the curtain along the upper and lower
edges of the hem. Tie the ribbon tails
into a bow.

All four edges of this
curtain are simply
hemmed by either
topstitching or fusing
them in place.
Construct the tabs by
fusing the seam, but
sew them to the
curtain for added
security. Team the
shower curtain with a
plastic liner to keep it
dry.

RUCHED RIBBON TOWEL

For a stylish bathroom, trim plain towels by sewing on wide ribbon and twisted cord.

C H E C K L I S T

Materials

Bath towel
Wide ribbon or lace
Twisted furnishing cord

Techniques

Machine stitching   pp. 22–23

Measuring up

Measure the width of the towel.

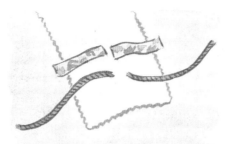

1 Cut two pieces of ribbon equal to half the measured width of the towel plus 2.5cm (1in). Cut two lengths of cord equal to half the measured width of the towel plus 30cm (12in).

2 On one end of each ribbon, turn under and press 2.5cm (1in). Tuck the cut edge in to meet the fold and press again. Sew the second fold in place by hand or machine.

3 On the other ends, turn under and press 1.2cm (½in).

4 Pin the two pieces of ribbon to the towel, covering the transition border and placing the pressed, unstitched ends even with the sides. There should be a gap of about 2.5cm (1in) at the centre. Stitch the long edges, backstitching at the inside ends to secure. This type of stitching is much quicker by machine.

5 On the outside ends, measure and mark the ribbon 1.2cm (½in) from the fold. Attach a safety pin to one end of a twisted cord. Insert the cord into the casing formed by the ribbon until the end of the cord is even with the side edge of the towel. Following the marked line, stitch the ribbon to the towel through the cord, backstitching in the area of the cord to secure. Trim the cord 5mm (¼in) from the end. Repeat for the remaining cord.

6 Sew the ribbon ends to the towel along the outside fold.

7 Pull the cords gently to gather the towel. Tie the cords into a bow and knot the cord ends.

If you mix and match ribbon and cord, the possibilities are endless. By adding the same trimmings to the curtains in your bathroom you could create a beautifully coordinated effect.

BEACH BLANKET

Transform an ordinary blanket into something special by adding a coordinating fabric border.

C H E C K L I S T

Materials

Furnishing fabric featuring printed motifs
Blanket
General sewing equipment
Paper-backed fusing web

Techniques

Machine stitching	pp. 22–23
Hand stitching	pp. 22–23
Fusing fabrics	pp. 24–25

Measuring up

Measure the width and length of the blanket.

Cutting sizes

Side Borders For the cutting length, add 2.5cm (1in) to the length of the blanket.
End Borders For the cutting length, add 2.5cm (1in) to the width of the blanket.
All Borders The cutting width is 28cm (11in). Piece several fabric widths together, if necessary, to get the right cutting lengths. Cutting sizes include 1.2cm (½in) seam allowance.

1 Following the cutting dimensions, cut two side borders and two end borders.

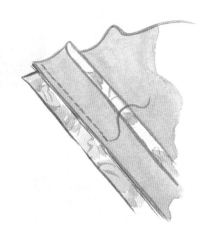

2 Cut several motifs from the fabric, allowing a margin of at least 1.2cm (½in) around the motif and making straight cuts, rather than attempting to follow the shapes closely. Place fusing web, paper side up, over the wrong side of each motif, and trace the cut edges. Cut the shape from the web. Pin each motif and the corresponding web shape together and set aside.

5 Pin one side border to one side edge of the blanket, right sides together, placing the unfolded edge on the marked line and the folded edge towards the centre of the blanket. Allow the border ends to overlap the top and bottom edges of the blanket by 1.2cm (½in). Following the stitching line on the border, stitch it to the blanket. Repeat with the other side border.

3 On the right side of the blanket mark a line 11.5cm (4½in) from the edge on all sides.

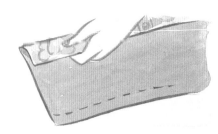

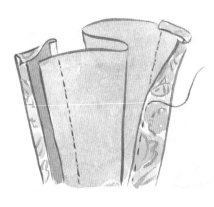

4 Turn under and press 1.2cm (½in) on one long edge of each border piece. On the other long edge, on the wrong side of the fabric, mark a stitching line 1.2cm (½in) from the edge.

6 Fold in the short ends of the borders even with the top and bottom edges of the blanket. Then fold each border in half lengthwise over the side edges of the blanket, matching the long folded edge to the line of stitching on the wrong side of the blanket. Topstitch through all layers, or use slipstitch to sew the folded edge in place.

7 ▶ Pin the two end borders to the top and bottom edges of the blanket, in the same way as for the side border. Allow 1.2cm (½in) of the border to extend past the edge of the blanket. Following the stitching line, stitch the borders in place, beginning and ending with backstitching at the inner corners where the adjacent borders meet.

8 ▶ Fold in the ends of the border even with the side edges of the blanket. Fold the borders over the

edges of the blanket, matching the long folded edge to the line of stitching on the wrong side of the blanket. Topstitch through all layers, or use slipstitch to sew the folded edge in place, beginning and ending at the inner corners where the borders meet.

9 ▶ On the right side, tuck under the points of the end borders to create a mitred corner. The fold should extend from the outer to the inner corner. Trim the point if necessary to reduce bulk. Repeat on the wrong side of the blanket.

10 ▶ Slipstitch the fold in place on the right and wrong sides of the border.

To complete the appliqués:

11 ▶ Following the manufacturer's instructions, iron each fusing web piece to the wrong side of the corresponding motif. Trim the appliqué carefully along the edge of the motif. Remove the paper backing, and apply the motifs to the blanket.

To make a whole beach ensemble, fuse some of these motifs to a beach umbrella or on to the picnic basket on page 34.

Select attractive motifs from the fabric and apply them using fusing web.

TEMPLATES

The templates on the following pages can be used for the appliqué shapes required for the Appliquéd picnic basket (page 34), the Pillowcase café curtains (page 40) and the Beach blanket (page 118). Or use your own designs. Each needs to be applied with paper-backed fusing web. This can be used in different ways (see the individual project instructions). Note that you will need to make separate tracings for the leaves and for the shaded parts of the Beach blanket motifs. The latter can then be applied on top of the complete shape. If the design needs to be enlarged or reduced, use either a larger or smaller grid than the one here, and transfer the designs accordingly.

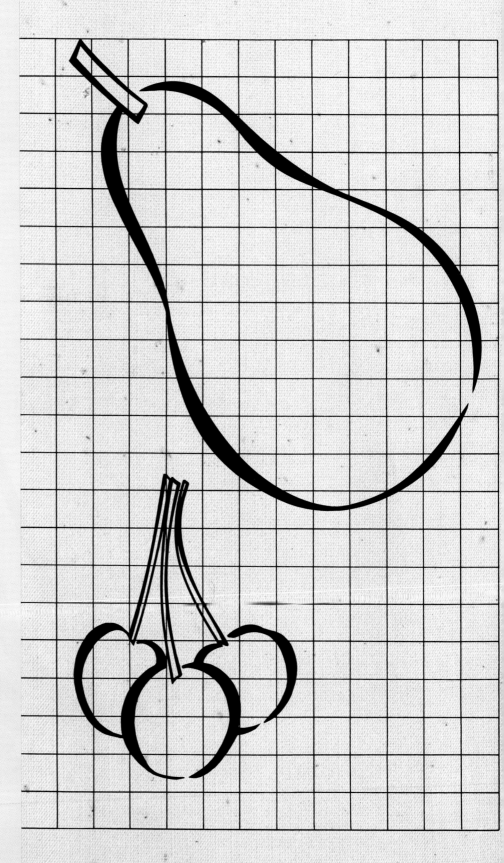

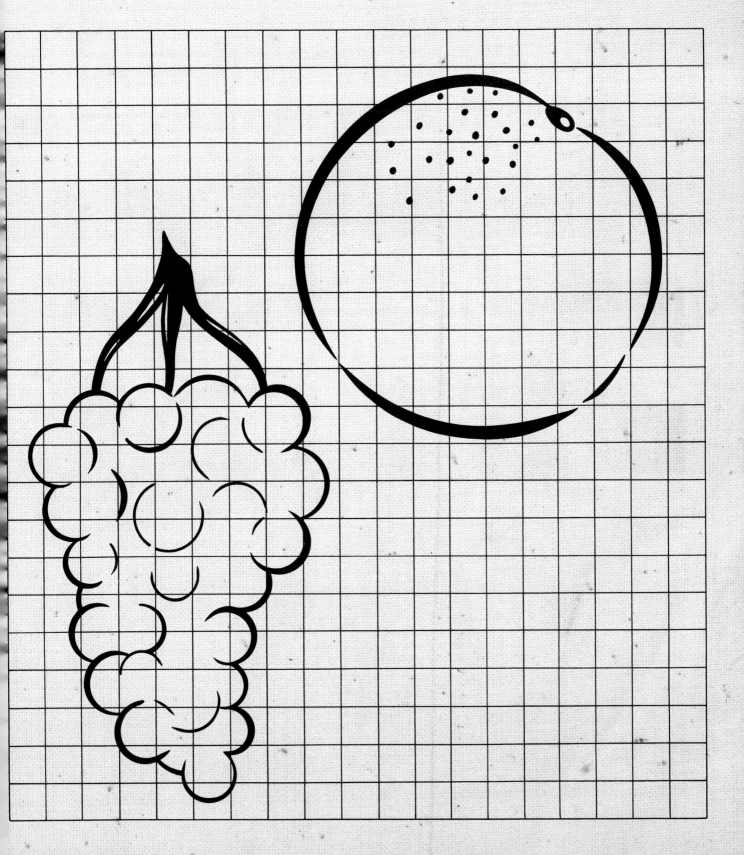

INDEX

Page numbers in italics refer to illustrations.

Acknowledgments

**The author would like to thank the following people and companies for
their contribution:**

For sharing their creative sewing and painting talents:

Christine Ben, Julia Bernstein, Millie Caltagirone, Susan Gill, Linda Heimer,
Nancy Keller, Artis Nolan, Sheila Zent and the staff of
Murdock Country Creations.

For the sewing notions, interfacings, fusibles, and fillers:

Dritz Corp., Freudenberg Pellon, Fairfield Processing Corp.

For the colorful trimmings, ribbon and laces:

Hollywood Trims Inc., C.M. Offray and Son Inc., William E. Wright Co.,
Wimpole Street Creations

For the decorative curtain rods:

Kirsch Division, Cooper Industries, Inc.

For the hand-crafted picnic basket, wooden stool, quilt rack and room
divider screen:

The Longaberger Company p. 34

Walnut Hollow Farm, Inc. pp. 48, 64

For the luscious terry cloth towels and the versatile bed linens:

Dundee Mills Inc., pp. 114, 116; Wamsutta, pp. 40, 70, 112

For the beautiful fabrics which provided so much of the inspiration:

Concord Fabrics of America, pp. 32, 62

Covington Fabrics Corp., pp. 52, 56, 82, 84, 104, 108, 110, 118

Cyrus Clark Co. Inc., pp. 86, 88

Pierre Deux, pp. 30, 39, 54, 66, 88, 100, 114

Richloom Fabrics Group available at Calico Corners, pp. 50, 64, 74, 95, 96

Springs Industries, Inc., pp. 58, 76, 92

VIP Fabrics, pp. 34, 94

For providing pictures used in this book, Quarto would like to thank
Next Interiors (page 7, below) and Arthur Sanderson and Sons Ltd., London
(page 8, left and page 9, right).
All other photographs are the copyright of Quarto Publishing.

We would also like to acknowledge the help of the following who kindly
loaned props for the purposes of photography: the Conran Shop, London
(chair, page 29); Elizabeth David Cookshop, London (copper jelly molds, page
41); The House of Steel, London (bedhead, pages 89 and 109);
Next Interiors, Leicester (crook curtain rail, pages 41, 59 and 63);
Purves & Purves, London (standard lamp, pages 43, 47 and 101);
Villeroy and Boch, London (china, silver and glasses, page 29).
Additional thanks to Judith Blacklock for her flower arrangements and
Ron Carolissen for slipcovers.